TEACHER'S PET PUBLICATIONS

LITPLAN TEACHER PACK
for
A Wrinkle in Time
based on the book by
Madeline L'Engle

Written by
Mary B. Collins

© 1996 Teacher's Pet Publications
All Rights Reserved

ISBN 978-1-60249-275-2

This **LitPlan** for Madeline L'Engle's
A Wrinkle in Time
has been brought to you by Teacher's Pet Publications, Inc.

Copyright Teacher's Pet Publications 1996
11504 Hammock Point
Berlin MD 21811

Only the student materials in this unit plan
such as worksheets, study questions, assignment sheets, and tests
may be reproduced multiple times for use in the purchaser's classroom.

For any additional copyright questions,
contact Teacher's Pet Publications.

www.tpet.com

TABLE OF CONTENTS - *A Wrinkle in Time*

Introduction	5
Unit Objectives	7
Reading Assignment Sheet	8
Unit Outline	9
Study Questions (Short Answer)	13
Quiz/Study Questions (Multiple Choice)	19
Pre-reading Vocabulary Worksheets	31
Lesson One (Introductory Lesson)	47
Nonfiction Assignment Sheet	49
Oral Reading Evaluation Form	51
Writing Assignment 1	56
Writing Assignment 2	66
Writing Assignment 3	67
Writing Evaluation Form	68
Vocabulary Review Activities	60
Extra Writing Assignments/Discussion ?s	58
Unit Review Activities	70
Unit Tests	73
Unit Resource Materials	103
Vocabulary Resource Materials	115

ABOUT THE AUTHOR
Madeleine L'Engle

L'ENGLE, MADELEINE (born 1918), U.S. author, actress, and teacher, born on November 29, 1918, in New York City. L'Engle came into prominence with her 1962 novel 'A Wrinkle in Time', which won the 1963 Newbery Medal. The novel is a science fiction story with philosophical and religious elements.

L'Engle received an A. B. degree in 1941 from Smith College and later studied at Columbia University. She acted in the theater in the 1940's and taught at private grade schools in New York. L'Engle's 'A Wrinkle in Time' and many of her other books pit good against evil while interweaving elements of fantasy and philosophy. These included two sequels to 'A Wrinkle in Time' -- 'A Wind in the Door' (1973) and 'A Swiftly Tilting Planet' (1978) -- and 'Camilla Dickinson' (1951), 'The Moon By Night' (1963), 'The Young Unicorns' (1968), 'Dragons in the Waters' (1976), and 'A Ring of Endless Light' (1980).

Among her volumes of poetry were 'Lines Scribbled on an Envelope' (1969), and 'The Weather of the Heart' (1978). She also published a series of autobiographical works based on her journals, including 'The Summer of the Great-Grandmother' (1974) and 'The Irrational Season' (1977).

In 1980 L'Engle won the American Book Award for 'A Swiftly Tilting Planet', and in 1981 'A Ring of Endless Light' was named a Newbery honor book. L'Engle had a following of loyal readers who were drawn by her imaginative and wide-ranging tales that were filled with symbols and elaborate plot twists.

---- Courtesy of Compton's Learning Company

INTRODUCTION

This unit has been designed to develop students' reading, writing, thinking, and language skills through exercises and activities related to *A Wrinkle in Time* by L'Engle. It includes twenty lessons, supported by extra resource materials.

The **introductory lesson** introduces students to one main theme of the novel through a bulletin board activity. Following the introductory activity, students are given a transition to explain how the activity relates to the book they are about to read. Following the transition, students are given the materials they will be using during the unit.

The **reading assignments** are approximately thirty pages each; some are a little shorter while others are a little longer. Students have approximately 15 minutes of pre-reading work to do prior to each reading assignment. This pre-reading work involves reviewing the study questions for the assignment and doing some vocabulary work for 8 to 10 vocabulary words they will encounter in their reading.

The **study guide questions** are fact-based questions; students can find the answers to these questions right in the text. These questions come in two formats: short answer or multiple choice The best use of these materials is probably to use the short answer version of the questions as study guides for students (since answers will be more complete), and to use the multiple choice version for occasional quizzes. If your school has the appropriate equipment, it might be a good idea to make transparencies of your answer keys for the overhead projector.

The **vocabulary work** is intended to enrich students' vocabularies as well as to aid in the students' understanding of the book. Prior to each reading assignment, students will complete a two-part worksheet for approximately 8 to 10 vocabulary words in the upcoming reading assignment. Part I focuses on students' use of general knowledge and contextual clues by giving the sentence in which the word appears in the text. Students are then to write down what they think the words mean based on the words' usage. Part II nails down the definitions of the words by giving students dictionary definitions of the words and having students match the words to the correct definitions based on the words' contextual usage. Students should then have an understanding of the words when they meet them in the text.

After each reading assignment, students will go back and formulate answers for the study guide questions. Discussion of these questions serves as a **review** of the most important events and ideas presented in the reading assignments.

A lesson is devoted to the **extra discussion questions/writing assignments**. These questions focus on interpretation, critical analysis and personal response, employing a variety of thinking skills and adding to the students' understanding of the novel.

Following the discussion of the novel, there is a **vocabulary review** lesson which pulls together all of the fragmented vocabulary lists for the reading assignments and gives students a review of all of the words they have studied.

There is a **group activity** that will have students working in small groups to create alien worlds.

There are three **writing assignments** in this unit, each with the purpose of informing, persuading, or having students express personal opinions. The first assignment is to inform: students research biographical information about the "fighters" mentioned in the book and others the class brainstorms. The second assignment is to persuade: students create travel brochures persuading people to come visit their alien worlds. The third assignment is to express personal opinions: students give their own views on one of the many ideas and themes presented in the book.

There is a **nonfiction reading assignment**. As students read the biographical information for their research projects, students will fill out a worksheet on which they answer questions regarding facts, interpretation, criticism, and personal opinions. The reports about the biographies also serve as students' nonfiction reading reports in this unit.

The **review lesson** pulls together all of the aspects of the unit. The teacher is given four or five choices of activities or games to use which all serve the same basic function of reviewing all of the information presented in the unit.

The **unit test** comes in two formats: multiple choice or short answer. As a convenience, two different tests for each format have been included.

There are additional **support materials** included with this unit. The **extra activities section** includes suggestions for an in-class library, crossword and word search puzzles related to the novel, and extra vocabulary worksheets. There is a list of **bulletin board ideas** which gives the teacher suggestions for bulletin boards to go along with this unit. In addition, there is a list of **extra class activities** the teacher could choose from to enhance the unit or as a substitution for an exercise the teacher might feel is inappropriate for his/her class. **Answer keys** follow the **reproducible student materials**, which may be reproduced for use in the teacher's classroom without infringement of copyrights. No other portion of the unit may be reproduced without the written consent of Teacher's Pet Publications, Inc.

The **level** of this unit can be varied depending upon the criteria on which the individual assignments are graded, the teacher's expectations of his/her students in class discussions, and the formats chosen for the study guides, quizzes and test.

UNIT OBJECTIVES - *A Wrinkle in Time*

1. Through reading L'Engle's *A Wrinkle in Time*, students will consider various kinds of good and evil in the world and ways in which the evil may be combated.

2. Students will demonstrate their understanding of the text on four levels: factual, interpretive, critical and personal.

3. Students will explore different kinds of communication.

4. Students will consider the importance of individuality.

5. Students will study passages from the story to extract the themes and to further study the author's use of language.

6. Students will be given the opportunity to practice reading aloud and silently to improve their skills in each area.

7. Students will answer questions to demonstrate their knowledge and understanding of the main events and characters in *A Wrinkle in Time* as they relate to the author's theme development.

8. Students will enrich their vocabularies and improve their understanding of the novel through the vocabulary lessons prepared for use in conjunction with the novel.

9. The writing assignments in this unit are geared to several purposes:
    a. To have students demonstrate their abilities to inform, to persuade, or to express their own personal ideas
        Note: Students will demonstrate ability to write effectively to <u>inform</u> by developing and organizing facts to convey information. Students will demonstrate the ability to write effectively to <u>persuade</u> by selecting and organizing relevant information, establishing an argumentative purpose, and by designing an appropriate strategy for an identified audience. Students will demonstrate the ability to write effectively to <u>express personal ideas</u> by selecting a form and its appropriate elements.
    b. To check the students' reading comprehension
    c. To make students think about the ideas presented by the novel
    d. To encourage logical thinking
    e. To provide an opportunity to practice good grammar and improve students' use of the English language.

READING ASSIGNMENT SHEET - *A Wrinkle in Time*

Date Assigned	Reading Assignment (Chapters)	Completion Date
	1-2	
	3-4	
	5-6	
	7-10	

UNIT OUTLINE - *A Wrinkle in Time*

1 Introduction	2 PVR 1-2	3 Study ?s 1-2 PVR 3-4	4 Study ?s 3-4 Library PVR 5-6	5 Study ?s 5-6 Writing Assignment #1 PVR 7-10
6 Reports	7 Study ?s 7-10 Reports	8 PVR 11-12	9 Study ?s 11-12 Extra Discussion Questions	10 Discussion
11 Vocabulary	12 Quotations	13 Group Work	14 Group Work	15 Writing Assignment 2

Key: P = Preview Study Questions   V = Vocabulary Work   R = Read

STUDY GUIDE QUESTIONS

STUDY GUIDE QUESTIONS - *A Wrinkle in Time*

Chapters 1-2
1. Identify and describe Meg, Mrs. Murry, Charles Wallace, and Mrs. Whatsit.
2. How did Mrs. Murry react when Mrs. Whatsit said, "There is such a thing as a tesseract"?
3. What did Mrs. Whatsit do that made Charles Wallace scold her?
4. Who is Calvin O'Keefe?
5. Why does Calvin call Charles a moron?
6. What does Calvin look like?
7. Who is Mrs. Who?
8. How does Calvin feel about going to the Murrys' house?

Chapters 3-4
1. How does Calvin feel about his family?
2. What is Meg's nickname?
3. What does Mrs. Murry say is Charles Wallace's difference?
4. What is the rumor about Mr. Murry?
5. Who is Mrs. Which?
6. Why was Meg terrified in the beginning of this chapter?
7. Describe the place where the three W's and the kids landed.
8. Into what being did Mrs. Whatsit change?
9. For what were the "flowers" used?
10. What did the Black Thing look like?

Chapters 5-6
1. Why were the children unable to function properly on the two-dimensional planet?
2. Why won't Mrs. Murry be worried about Meg and Charles Wallace?
3. Who is the Happy Medium?
4. What happens when a star dies in battle with the Black Thing?
5. What does Camazotz feel like?
6. Why is the danger greatest for Charles Wallace?
7. How were the children on Camazotz playing?
8. What were the people of Camazotz like?

Wrinkle Short Answer Study Questions Page 2

Chapters 7-10
1. What did the man the children met in CENTRAL Central do?
2. What did the man on the chair want to do?
3. Why doesn't the imitation meal taste good to Charles Wallace?
4. Why does Charles Wallace finally allow himself to be hypnotized?
5. What happens when someone on Camazotz has a cold?
6. What is IT?
7. How did Meg use her faults?
8. How did Meg get in to see her father?
9. How did Mr. Murry get Calvin, Meg, and himself out of IT's domain?
10. Why is Meg angry at her father?

Chapters 11-12
1. What are the creatures on Ixchel like?
2. What does Meg call the one creature who takes care of her?
3. Is Ixchel a dark planet?
4. Why is Meg the only one who can go to save Charles Wallace?
5. To what does Mrs. Whatsit compare human lives?
6. What does Meg have that IT doesn't have?
7. What did Meg do to get Charles Wallace away from IT?

KEY: STUDY GUIDE QUESTIONS - *A Wrinkle in Time*

Chapters 1-2

1. Identify and describe Meg, Mrs. Murry, Charles Wallace, and Mrs. Whatsit.

   Meg - Meg is Mr. and Mrs. Murry's daughter. She is a poor student and a bit of a misfit, but she is smart.

   Mrs. Murry - She is the mother of Meg, Charles Wallace, Sandy, and Dennys. She is calm, kind, beautiful, and smart.

   Charles Wallace - Charles Wallace is Meg's brother. Although he is very smart, he is rumored to be "slow" among the other kids. He has a special talent of being able to probe people's minds.

   Mrs. Whatsit - Mrs. Whatsit is very different. She dresses like a tramp and seems to have psychic powers.

2. How did Mrs. Murry react when Mrs. Whatsit said, "There is such a thing as a tesseract"?

   She got very nervous and turned very white.

3. What did Mrs. Whatsit do that made Charles Wallace scold her?

   She stole Mrs. Buncombe's sheets.

4. Who is Calvin O'Keefe?

   He is a boy Meg and Charles meet in the woods near their home. Charles thinks that Calvin is like him, in the sense that he is very smart and also able to tell what people are thinking.

5. Why does Calvin call Charles a moron?

   He calls him a moron because he was "preconditioned in the concept of his mentality." In other words, other people called Charles a moron, so Calvin assumed that it was true.

6. What does Calvin look like?

   He has orange hair that needs cutting. He is very tall and skinny to the point that his bones stick out of his wrists. He has unusual, bright blue eyes.

7. Who is Mrs. Who?

   Mrs. Who is a friend of Mrs. Whatsit. She has thick spectacles. She has memorized many different quotes in several different languages and uses them to communicate her thoughts.

8. How does Calvin feel about going to the Murrys' house?

   He feels very comfortable and says, "I have the funniest feeling that for the first time in my life I am going home!"

Chapters 3-4
1. How does Calvin feel about his family?
>He loves them very much, but he feels that they do not care for him.

2. What is Meg's nickname?
>Her nickname is "Megaparsec," which also refers to 3.26 million light years.

3. What does Mrs. Murry say is Charles Wallace's difference?
>She refers to Charles Wallace's difference as being in essence, not physical.

4. What is the rumor about Mr. Murry?
>Some people said he left his family and went off with another woman.

5. Who is Mrs. Which?
>She is another friend of Mrs. Whatsit. She speaks in a strange way.

6. Why was Meg terrified in the beginning of this chapter?
>During the "traveling" she couldn't feel her body, hear anything, or see anything, just as if she were in a void.

7. Describe the place where the three W's and the kids landed.
>It was beautiful. The air was soft and sweet, and the grass was green, covered with beautiful flowers.

8. Into what being did Mrs. Whatsit change?
>She changed into a creature something like a centaur, with a much more noble body and wings.

9. For what were the "flowers" used?
>The flowers acted like oxygen masks for the humans.

10. What did the Black Thing look like?
>It looked like a great, dark, evil shadow.

Chapters 5-6
1. Why were the children unable to function properly on the two-dimensional planet?
>There was no third dimension for their volume; they looked like cut-out paper dolls.

2. Why won't Mrs. Murry be worried about Meg and Charles Wallace?
>The Mrs. W's made a time wrinkle so the children will arrive home five minutes before they left.

3. Who is the Happy Medium?
   She showed the children Earth, which was surrounded by the Black Thing.

4. What happens when a star dies in battle with the Black Thing?
   It becomes a person like Mrs. Whatsit.

5. What does Camazotz feel like?
   It feels like Earth with the same atmosphere, trees, hills, and physical features, but something seems different. (The children discover that the people are different, all doing the same things at the same time in the same way.)

6. Why is the danger greatest for Charles Wallace?
   He is the youngest and the most vulnerable. Also, his arrogance sometimes betrays him.

7. How were the children on Camazotz playing?
   They were playing ball and skipping rope, but they were doing it in rhythm. As the balls hit the ground, so did the jump ropes.

8. What were the people of Camazotz like?
   They always kept in perfect order, everyone and everything moved to a rhythm.

Chapters 7-10
1. What did the man the children met in CENTRAL Central do?
   The man ran a spelling machine on the second grade level.

2. What did the man on the chair want to do?
   He wanted to hypnotize the children.

3. Why doesn't the imitation meal taste good to Charles Wallace?
   He can't be hypnotized enough to be fooled.

4. Why does Charles Wallace finally allow himself to be hypnotized?
   He thought he could hold part of himself out and end his hypnotic state when he desired.

5. What happens when someone on Camazotz has a cold?
   They are simply put to sleep so they don't suffer.

6. What is IT?
   IT is a great big pulsating brain that controls everyone and everything that succumbs to it.

7. How did Meg use her faults?
   She became stubborn and refused to succumb to IT.

8. How did Meg get in to see her father?
   She used the glasses Mrs. W gave her.

9. How did Mr. Murry get Calvin, Meg and himself out of IT's domain?
   He and the children tessered.

10. Why is Meg angry at her father?
    She blames him for messing up and sending them to strange planet.

<u>Chapters 11-12</u>
1. What are the creatures on Ixchel like?
   They are kind, gentle beings who want to take care of their three visitors.

2. What does Meg call the one creature who takes care of her?
   She calls her Aunt Beast.

3. Is Ixchel a dark planet?
   No.

4. Why is Meg the only one who can go to save Charles Wallace?
   They understand each other, and she has known him the longest; therefore, she has the best chance of reaching him.

5. To what does Mrs. Whatsit compare human lives?
   She compares them to a sonnet. Each has a strict form but freedom within that form.

6. What does Meg have that IT doesn't have?
   She has love.

7. What did Meg do to get Charles Wallace away from IT?
   She used her love to get him out.

MULTIPLE CHOICE STUDY GUIDE/QUIZ QUESTIONS - *A Wrinkle in Time*

Chapters 1-2

1. Identify and describe Meg, Mrs. Murry, Charles Wallace, and Mrs. Whatsit.

    __ Meg   A. Mother

    __ Mrs. Murry   B. Has a special talent of being able to probe people's minds

    __ Charles Wallace C. Poor Student, bit of a misfit, but smart

    __ Mrs. Whatsit   D. Dresses like a tramp; seems to have psychic powers

2. How did Mrs. Murry react when Mrs. Whatsit said, "There is such a thing as a tesseract"?
    a. She laughed.
    b. She burst into tears.
    c. She smiled and nodded knowingly.
    d. She got nervous and turned very white.

3. What did Mrs. Whatsit do that made Charles Wallace scold her?
    a. She insulted his mother.
    b. She stole Mrs. Buncombe's sheets.
    c. She interrupted him.
    d. She called him a moron.

4. Who is Calvin O'Keefe?
    a. He is a boy Meg and Cal meet in the woods near their home.
    b. He is Mrs. Whatsit's nephew.
    c. He is Charles Wallace's best friend from school.
    d. He is Meg and Charles Wallace's brother.

5. Why does Calvin call Charles a moron?
    a. He is angry at Charles Wallace.
    b. Charles Wallace is not very bright.
    c. He was preconditioned in the concept of his mentality.
    d. He was trying to make himself look more important.

6. What does Calvin look like?
    a. Brown hair, tall, and skinny
    b. Brown hair and strange orangeish eyes
    c. Brown hair and strange blue eyes
    d. Orange hair, tall, and skinny

Wrinkle Multiple Choice Study Questions Page 2

7. Who is Mrs. Who?
    a. She is a friend of Mrs. Whatsit.
    b. She wears thick glasses.
    c. She speaks in quotations.
    d. All of the above

8. How does Calvin feel about going to the Murrys' house?
    a. He feels like it's home.
    b. He's a little afraid.
    c. He's curious.
    d. He doesn't want to go.

Wrinkle Multiple Choice Study Questions Page 3

<u>Chapters 3-4</u>
1. How does Calvin feel about his family?
    a. He loves them but thinks they don't care for him.
    b. He doesn't care for them.
    c. He thinks they're all crazy.
    d. He thinks they're all morons.

2. What is Meg's nickname?
    a. Megatron
    b. Megalopolis
    c. Megaparsec
    d. Megasecond

3. What does Mrs. Murry say is Charles Wallace's difference?
    a. He is far more intelligent than most other people on Earth.
    b. He is different in essence, not physically.
    c. He is telepathic.
    d. He is more sensitive and has an overactive imagination.

4. What is the rumor about Mr. Murry?
    a. He was killed in a government scientific experiment.
    b. He was picked up by aliens.
    c. He was severely mutilated in a science experiment.
    d. He has gone off with another woman.

5. Who is Mrs. Which?
    a. A witch
    b. A friend of Mrs. Whatsit and Mrs. Who
    c. A neighbor
    d. A friend of Mrs. Murry

6. Why was Meg terrified in the beginning of this chapter?
    a. She had a nightmare.
    b. Mrs. Who scared her.
    c. "Traveling" scared her.
    d. She was shoved through a wall of glass.

Wrinkle Multiple Choice Study Questions Page 4

7. Describe the place where the three W's and the kids landed.
   a. Stale air, rocky terrain, and colorless
   b. Sweet air, green grass, beautiful flowers
   c. Everything looked as if a shadow were over it.
   d. It was as if they were in a void.

8. Into what being did Mrs. Whatsit change?
   a. Winged angel
   b. Butterfly
   c. Horse
   d. Centaur

9. For what were the "flowers" used?
   a. To help the humans breathe
   b. As a sleeping potion
   c. As food
   d. To help them tesser

10. What did the Black Thing look like?
    a. A centaur
    b. A great, dark, evil shadow
    c. A frowning jack-o-lantern
    d. A black hole

Wrinkle Multiple Choice Study Questions Page 5

Chapters 5-6

1. Why were the children unable to function properly on the two-dimensional planet?
    a. There wasn't enough oxygen.
    b. They never completely recomposed.
    c. They were like paper dolls.
    d. The Black Thing had taken hold of them.

2. Why won't Mrs. Murry be worried about Meg and Charles Wallace?
    a. She thinks they've gone to a movie.
    b. She knows they won't get into trouble.
    c. She trusts the Mrs. W's.
    d. She'll think they've only been gone five minutes.

3. Who is the Happy Medium?
    a. She tried to exercise the Black Thing.
    b. She contacted their dead father.
    c. She showed the children Earth surrounded by the Black Thing.
    d. It was through the Happy Medium that they were able to tesser.

4. What happens when a star dies in battle with the Black Thing?
    a. It goes out.
    b. It becomes an angel.
    c. It becomes like Mrs. Whatsit.
    d. It turns black.

5. How was Camazotz different from Earth?
    a. It was much prettier.
    b. All the people did the same things at the same time in the same way.
    c. The people used flowers to help them breathe.
    d. It was dark; there was no sunlight.

6. Why is the danger greatest for Charles Wallace?
    a. He is the youngest and most vulnerable.
    b. He is the smartest.
    c. He is the smallest.
    d. His special mind reading skills put him at risk.

Wrinkle Multiple Choice Study Questions Page 6

7. How were the children on Camazotz playing?
    a. They played in pairs.
    b. They played in rhythm.
    c. They sang while they played.
    d. They were all fighting.

8. What were the people of Camazotz like?
    a. Slovenly
    b. Unhappy
    c. Frightened
    d. In perfect order

Wrinkle Multiple Choice Study Questions Page 7

<u>Chapters 7-10</u>
1. What did the man the children met in CENTRAL Central do?
    a. Processed papers
    b. Guarded the wall
    c. Ran a moving sidewalk
    d. Ran a second grade spelling machine

2. What did the man on the chair want to do?
    a. Hypnotize the children
    b. Help the children find Meg's father
    c. Teach the children multiplication table
    d. Treat the children to a good meal to show his good will

3. Why doesn't the imitation meal taste good to Charles Wallace?
    a. It had a bad odor.
    b. He was too smart to eat it.
    c. He couldn't be hypnotized enough to be fooled.
    d. He was too upset.

4. Why does Charles Wallace finally allow himself to be hypnotized?
    a. It was the only way to find his father.
    b. He thought he could get out of the hypnosis whenever he wanted.
    c. He was tricked into it.
    d. Meg asked him to.

5. What happens when someone on Camazotz has a cold?
    a. They are given a pill that relieves the symptoms.
    b. They are "put to sleep" so they don't suffer.
    c. They are put in an isolation chamber.
    d. They are hypnotized.

6. What is IT?
    a. Big pulsating brain that controls everything that succumbs to it
    b. A government experiment gone wrong
    c. God
    d. Mr. Murry

Wrinkle Multiple Choice Study Questions Page 8

7. How did Meg use her faults?
    a. She became stubborn and refused to succumb to IT.
    b. She chattered incessantly to avoid IT
    c. She got angry and punched IT in the face.
    d. She became impatient and punched IT in the face.

8. How did Meg get in to see her father?
    a. She bribed IT.
    b. She thought the right thoughts.
    c. She broke in.
    d. She used the glasses Mrs. W. gave her.

9. How did Mr. Murry get Calvin, Meg, and himself out of IT's domain?
    a. They used a secret passage he remembered.
    b. He and the children tessered.
    c. They used Mrs. W's glasses.
    d. They thought themselves out of it.

10. Why is Meg angry at her father?
    a. He broke her glasses.
    b. He never explained why he left home.
    c. He left Calvin behind.
    d. She blames him for messing up and sending them to a strange planet.

Wrinkle Multiple Choice Study Questions Page 9

Chapters 11-12

1. What are the creatures on Ixchel like?
    a. They are small ITs.
    b. They've been taken over by the Black Thing.
    c. They are kind and gentle.
    d. They are distant and suspicious.

2. What does Meg call the one creature who takes care of her?
    a. Mother Beast
    b. Gentle beast
    c. Aunt Ixchel
    d. Aunt Beast

3. Why is Meg the only one who can go to save Charles Wallace?
    a. Only she knows the way.
    b. She understands him the best.
    c. The glasses will only work for her.
    d. IT won't suspect her.

4. To what does Mrs. Whatsit compare human lives?
    a. A sonnet
    b. A song
    c. A bird
    d. Morning light

5. What does Meg have that IT doesn't have?
    a. Intelligence
    b. Patience
    c. Love
    d. Knowledge

6. What did Meg use to get Charles Wallace away from IT?
    a. Light
    b. Poetry
    c. Mathematics
    d. Love

ANSWER KEY MULTIPLE CHOICE STUDY/QUIZ QUESTIONS
A Wrinkle in Time

Chapters 1-2	**Chapters 3-4**	**Chapters 5-6**	**Chapters 7-10**
1. C A B D	1. A	1. C	1. D
2. D	2. C	2. D	2. A
3. B	3. B	3. C	3. C
4. A	4. D	4. C	4. B
5. C	5. B	5. B	5. B
6. D	6. C	6. A	6. A
7. D	7. B	7. B	7. A
8. A	8. D	8. C	8. D
	9. A		9. B
	10. B		10. D

Chapters 11-12
1. C
2. D
3. B
4. C
5. C
6. D

PREREADING VOCABULARY WORKSHEETS

VOCABULARY - *A Wrinkle in Time*

<u>Chapters 1-2</u> Part I: Using Prior Knowledge and Contextual Clues

    Below are the sentences in which the vocabulary words appear in the text. Read the sentence. Use any clues you can find in the sentence combined with your prior knowledge, and write what you think the underlined words mean in the space provided.

1. Surely her mother must know what people were saying, must be aware of the smugly <u>vicious</u> gossip.

2. Nothing ruffled the <u>serenity</u> of her expression.

3. Charles Wallace began to speak, suddenly, with none of the usual baby <u>preliminaries</u> using entire sentences.

4. At last Meg looked at him, pushing at her glasses a characteristic <u>gesture</u>

5. ... behind Mr. Jenkins' surface concern was a gleam of <u>avid</u> curiosity.

6. Charles Wallace slipped his hand <u>confidingly</u> in Meg's, and the sweet, little-boy gesture warmed her...

7. You tell me, you see, sort of inad---<u>inadvertently</u>.

8. "I might ask the same of you, " the boy said with some <u>indignation</u>.

9. I need fuel so I can sort things out and <u>assimilate</u> them properly.

Vocabulary - *A Wrinkle in Time* Chapters 1-2

Part II: Determining the Meaning

You have tried to figure out the meanings of the vocabulary words for Chapters 1-2. Now match the vocabulary words to their dictionary definitions. If there are words for which you cannot figure out the definition by contextual clues and by process of elimination, look them up in a dictionary.

____ 1. vicious
____ 2. serenity
____ 3. preliminaries
____ 4. resentment
____ 5. gesture
____ 6. avid
____ 7. confidingly
____ 8. inadvertently
____ 9. indignation
____ 10. assimilate

A. enthusiastic; ardent
B. unintentionally; by accident
C. anger aroused by something mean, unjust or unworthy
D. to absorb and incorporate
E. comfortingly; seeking or giving confidence
F. spiteful, malicious
G. a motion of the limbs or \body
H. tranquility
I. preparation
J. indignation or ill-will felt as a result of some offense

Vocabulary - *A Wrinkle in Time* Chapters 3-4

Part I: Using Prior Knowledge and Contextual Clues
    Below are the sentences in which the vocabulary words appear in the text. Read the sentence. Use any clues you can find in the sentence combined with your prior knowledge, and write what you think the underlined words mean in the space provided.

1. "It might also help if Meg's handwriting were legible," Mrs. Murry said. "With a good deal of difficult I can usually decipher it...

2. "Yah," Meg said dubiously.

3. ...and with a deft gesture took the sheet and folded it.

4. ...and feeling the gentle, inexorable tug of the moon.

5. Mrs. Which, despite her looks and ephemeral broomstick, was someone in whom one could put complete trust.

6. ...and at something in her voice Meg felt prickles of apprehension.

7. You can't go on changing my name each time I metamorphose.

8. It seemed completely incomprehensible that through this bliss could come the faintest whisper of doubt.

9. The dark shadow was still there. It had not lessened or dispersed with the coming of night.

10. ...the shadow was behind them, so that they saw only the stars unobscured.

Vocabulary - *A Wrinkle in Time* Chapters 3-4 Continued

Part II: Determining the Meaning

You have tried to figure out the meanings of the vocabulary words for Chapters 3-4. Now match the vocabulary words to their dictionary definitions. If there are words for which you cannot figure out the definition by contextual clues and by process of elimination, look them up in a dictionary.

____ 1. decipher   A. short-lived; lasting only a brief time
____ 2. dubiously   B. decode; to read or interpret
____ 3. deft   C. change in form; transform
____ 4. inexorable   D. dread; uneasy anticipation
____ 5. ephemeral   E. doubtfully
____ 6. apprehension   F. serene happiness
____ 7. metamorphose   G. become less dense by scattering; dispelled
____ 8. bliss   H. skillful
____ 9. dispersed   I. unyielding
____ 10. unobscured   J. not obstructed; in full view

Vocabulary - *A Wrinkle in Time* Chapters 5-6

Part I: Using Prior Knowledge and Contextual Clues

    Below are the sentences in which the vocabulary words appear in the text. Read the sentence. Use any clues you can find in the sentence combined with your prior knowledge, and write what you think the underlined words mean in the space provided.

1. We will go first and take you afterward in the <u>backwash</u>.

2. ... she was prepared for the sudden and complete <u>dissolution</u> of her body.

3. The relief from the <u>intolerable</u> pressure was all she needed.

4. Mrs. Whatsit looked hurt, but she <u>subsided</u>.

5. ... a thing that wanted to eat and digest her like some enormous <u>malignant</u> beast of prey.

6. You will just have to wait until the <u>propitious</u> moment.

7. ... sometimes dropping it and running after it with awkward <u>furtive</u> leaps. Meg's reassurance came quickly. "You'll know him! Of course you'll know him.

Vocabulary - *A Wrinkle in Time* Chapters 5-6 Continued

Part II: Determining the Meaning

You have tried to figure out the meanings of the vocabulary words for Chapters 5-6. Now match the vocabulary words to their dictionary definitions. If there are words for which you cannot figure out the definition by contextual clues and by process of elimination, look them up in a dictionary.

____ 1. backwash   A. actively evil in nature
____ 2. dissolution   B. abated; settled down; lessened
____ 3. intolerable   C. presenting favorable circumstances
____ 4. subsided   D. something that restores confidence
____ 5. malignant   E. stealthy
____ 6. propitious   F. unbearable
____ 7. furtive   G. decomposition into fragments or parts
____ 8. reassurance   H. backward flow of air as from a propeller

Vocabulary - *A Wrinkle in Time* Chapters 7-8

Part I: Using Prior Knowledge and Contextual Clues

Below are the sentences in which the vocabulary words appear in the text. Read the sentence. Use any clues you can find in the sentence combined with your prior knowledge, and write what you think the underlined words mean in the space provided.

1. The men all wore nondescript business suits.

2. ... she had to look obliquely so that she was not sure exactly what the face really looked like.

3. Meg did not tell the man on the chair that patience was not one of her virtues.

4. She scowled down at the ground in sullen fury.

5. "Why are you being so belligerent and uncooperative?"

6. Fighting down her hysteria, Meg took Charles's other arm and held it tightly.

7. He spoke in his calmest, most reasonable voice, the voice which infuriated the twins.

8. "Merely another misconception.

9. It is so much kinder simply to annihilate anyone who is ill.

10. There was something ominous to Meg in the very compactness of the room, as though the walls, the ceiling, the floor might move together and crush anybody rash enough to enter.

Vocabulary - *A Wrinkle in Time* Chapters 7 - 8 Continued

Part II: Determining the Meaning

You have tried to figure out the meanings of the vocabulary words for Chapters 7 - 8. Now match the vocabulary words to their dictionary definitions. If there are words for which you cannot figure out the definition by contextual clues and by process of elimination, look them up in a dictionary.

____ 1. nondescript
____ 2. obliquely
____ 3. virtues
____ 4. fury
____ 5. belligerent
____ 6. hysteria
____ 7. infuriated
____ 8. misconception
____ 9. annihilate
____ 10. ominous

A. rage; violent anger
B. ordinary; has no outstanding features
C. wipe out
D. made angry
E. foreboding; portentous
F. good qualities
G. marked by hostile behavior
H. at a slant
I. excessive or uncontrollable fear or other emotion
J. incorrect understanding

Vocabulary - *A Wrinkle in Time* Chapters 9-10

Part I: Using Prior Knowledge and Contextual Clues

Below are the sentences in which the vocabulary words appear in the text. Read the sentence. Use any clues you can find in the sentence combined with your prior knowledge, and write what you think the underlined words mean in the space provided.

1. She seemed utterly alone, the silence and darkness <u>impenetrable</u> forever.

2. "You'll have to <u>defer</u> your explanations. Let's go."

3. "But he isn't Charles!" Meg cried in <u>anguish</u>.

4. Time on Camazotz seems to be <u>inverted</u>, turned in on itself.

5. But we did try very hard not to let it be known abroad that we were trying to make it <u>practicable</u>.

6. We can know this, but it's far more than we can understand with our <u>puny</u> little brains.

7. Charles Wallace was being devoured by IT, and her <u>omnipotent</u> father was doing nothing.

8. I am a human being, and a very <u>fallible</u> one.

9. ...and she felt a soft, tingling warmth go all through her that momentarily <u>assuaged</u> her pain.

Vocabulary - *A Wrinkle in Time* Chapters 9-10 Continued

Part II: Determining the Meaning

You have tried to figure out the meanings of the vocabulary words for Chapters 9-10. Now match the vocabulary words to their dictionary definitions. If there are words for which you cannot figure out the definition by contextual clues and by process of elimination, look them up in a dictionary.

____ 1. impenetrable
____ 2. defer
____ 3. anguish
____ 4. inverted
____ 5. practicable
____ 6. puny
____ 7. omnipotent
____ 8. fallible
____ 9. assuaged

A. turned upside down or wrong side out
B. all powerful
C. can make mistakes
D. small
E. put off to a later time
F. made less severe
G. can't be gone through
H. can be done; feasible
I. agonizing physical or mental pain

Vocabulary - *A Wrinkle in Time* Chapters 11-12

Part I: Using Prior Knowledge and Contextual Clues

    Below are the sentences in which the vocabulary words appear in the text. Read the sentence. Use any clues you can find in the sentence combined with your prior knowledge, and write what you think the underlined words mean.

1. ... with comparative freedom, and the pain was no longer so <u>acute</u>.

2. ... and her disappointment in her father's human fallibility rose like <u>gorge</u> in her throat.

3. Then she realized that this was <u>absurd</u>.

4. Most of the time all that <u>emanated</u> from them was gentle puzzlement.

5. <u>Appallingly</u>, Mrs. Whatsit voice was cold.

6. As Meg walked down the street all the lights were extinguished <u>simultaneously</u>.

7. She gasped for breath, for breath in her own rhythm, not the <u>permeating</u> pulsing of IT.

8. As she had seem him before, with a tic in his forehead <u>reiterating</u> the revolting rhythm of IT.

9. No, it was not anger, it was <u>loathing</u>, it was hatred, sheer and unadulterated.

10. No, it was not anger, it was loathing, it was hatred, sheer and <u>unadulterated.</u>

Vocabulary - *A Wrinkle in Time* Chapters 11-12 Continued

Part II: Determining the Meaning
 You have tried to figure out the meanings of the vocabulary words for Chapters 11-12. Now match the vocabulary words to their dictionary definitions. If there are words for which you cannot figure out the definition by contextual clues and by process of elimination, look them up in a dictionary.

___ 1. acute
___ 2. gorge
___ 3. absurd
___ 4. emanated
___ 5. appallingly
___ 6. simultaneously
___ 7. permeating
___ 8. reiterating
___ 9. loathing
___ 10. unadulterated

A. causing dismay
B. abhorrence; detesting
C. saying or doing the same thing again
D. at the same time
E. sharp; severe
F. originated; came from
G. a mass obstructing a narrow passage
H. not diluted; pure
I. spreading or flowing throughout
J. ridiculous

VOCABULARY ANSWER KEY - *A Wrinkle in Time*

Chapters 1-2	Chapters 3-4	Chapters 5-6	Chapters 7-8	Chapters 9-10	Chapters 11-12
1. F	1. B	1. H	1. B	1. G	1. E
2. H	2. E	2. G	2. H	2. E	2. G
3. I	3. H	3. F	3. F	3. I	3. J
4. J	4. I	4. B	4. A	4. A	4. F
5. G	5. A	5. A	5. G	5. H	5. A
6. A	6. D	6. C	6. I	6. D	6. D
7. E	7. C	7. E	7. D	7. B	7. I
8. B	8. F	8. D	8. J	8. C	8. C
9. C	9. G		9. C	9. F	9. B
10. D	10. J		10. E		10. H

DAILY LESSONS

LESSON ONE

Objectives
1. To introduce the unit.
2. To distribute books and other related materials

NOTE: Prior to this lesson, you need to tell students to bring with them to class an account of a strange event--a UFO sighting, an example of psychic powers, or anything which could not be explained by our current technology.

Also as prior preparation, you should put up the background paper and title for a bulletin board entitled A WRINKLE IN TIME: A LINK TO OTHER WORLDS? or some other suitable phrase. Leave space for students to post their pictures.

Activity #1
Ask students to clear their desks except for the articles they have brought to class. Have each student tell about his/her article and then let the student post it on the bulletin board.

Transition: In the book you are about to read, *A Wrinkle in Time*, many strange things happen as the main characters travel through time and space to strange worlds to find and rescue their father.

Activity #2
Distribute the materials students will use in this unit. Explain in detail how students are to use these materials.

Study Guides Students should read the study guide questions for each reading assignment prior to beginning the reading assignment to get a feeling for what events and ideas are important in the section they are about to read. After reading the section, students will (as a class or individually) answer the questions to review the important events and ideas from that section of the book. Students should keep the study guides as study materials for the unit test.

Vocabulary Prior to reading a reading assignment, students will do vocabulary work related to the section of the book they are about to read. Following the completion of the reading of the book, there will be a vocabulary review of all the words used in the vocabulary assignments. Students should keep their vocabulary work as study materials for the unit test.

Reading Assignment Sheet You need to fill in the reading assignment sheet to let students know by when their reading has to be completed. You can either write the assignment sheet up on a side blackboard or bulletin board and leave it there for students to see each day, or you can "ditto" copies for each student to have. In either case, you should advise students to become very familiar with the reading assignments so they know what is expected of them.

Extra Activities Center The resource sections of this unit contain suggestions for an extra library of related books and articles in your classroom as well as crossword and word search puzzles. Make an extra activities center in your room where you will keep these materials for students to use. (Bring the books and articles in from the library and keep several copies of the puzzles on hand.) Explain to students that these materials are available for students to use when they finish reading assignments or other class work early.

Nonfiction Assignment Sheet Explain to students that they each are to read at least one non-fiction piece from the in-class library at some time during the unit. Students will fill out a non-fiction assignment sheet after completing the reading to help you evaluate their reading experiences and to help the students think about and evaluate their own reading experiences.

Books Each school has its own rules and regulations regarding student use of school books. Advise students of the procedures that are normal for your school.

NONFICTION ASSIGNMENT SHEET
(To be completed after reading the required nonfiction article)

Name _____ Date _____

Title of Nonfiction Read _____

Written By _____ Publication Date _____

I. Factual Summary: Write a short summary of the piece you read.

II. Vocabulary
    1. With which vocabulary words in the piece did you encounter some degree of difficulty?

    2. How did you resolve your lack of understanding with these words?

III. Interpretation: What was the main point the author wanted you to get from reading his work?

IV. Criticism
    1. With which points of the piece did you agree or find easy to accept? Why?

    2. With which points of the piece did you disagree or find difficult to believe? Why?

V. Personal Response: What do you think about this piece? <u>OR</u> How does this piece influence your ideas?

LESSON TWO

Objectives
1. Preview the study questions and vocabulary for chapters 1-2
2. To read chapters 1-2
3. To give students practice reading orally
4. To evaluate students' oral reading

Activity #1

Show students how to preview the study questions and how to do the prereading vocabulary worksheet and then give them time to complete the worksheet.

Activity #2

Have students read chapters 1-2 of *A Wrinkle in Time* out loud in class. You probably know the best way to get readers with your class; pick students at random, ask for volunteers, or use whatever method works best for your group. If you have not yet completed an oral reading evaluation for your students this marking period, this would be a good opportunity to do so. A form is included with this unit for your convenience.

If students do not complete reading chapters 1-2 in class, they should do so prior to your next class meeting.

ORAL READING EVALUATION - *A Wrinkle in Time*

Name _____ Class _____ Date _____

SKILL	EXCELLENT	GOOD	AVERAGE	FAIR	POOR
Fluency	5	4	3	2	1
Clarity	5	4	3	2	1
Audibility	5	4	3	2	1
Pronunciation	5	4	3	2	1
_____	5	4	3	2	1
_____	5	4	3	2	1

Total _____ Grade _____

LESSON THREE

Objectives
    1. To review the main events and ideas from chapters 1-2
    2. To preview the study questions for chapters 3-4
    3. To familiarize students with the vocabulary in chapters 3-4
    4. To read chapters 3-4

Activity #1
    Give students a few minutes to formulate answers for the study guide questions for chapters 1-2 and then discuss the answers to the questions in detail. Write the answers on the board or overhead transparency so students can have the correct answers for study purposes.

    NOTE: It is a good practice in public speaking and leadership skills for individual students to take charge of leading the discussions of the study questions. Perhaps a different student could go to the front of the class and lead the discussion each day that the study questions are discussed during this unit. Of course, the teacher should guide the discussion when appropriate and be sure to fill in any gaps the students leave.

Activity #2
    Give students about fifteen minutes to preview the study questions for chapters 3-4 of *A Wrinkle in Time* and to do the related vocabulary work.

Activity #3
    Continue the oral reading evaluations while choosing students to read chapters 3-4 orally in class. If students do not complete this assignment in class, they should complete it prior to your next class meeting.

LESSON FOUR

Objectives
1. To review the main ideas and events from chapters 3-4
2. To preview the study questions and vocabulary for chapters 5-6
3. To read chapters 5-6
4. To make the nonfiction reading assignment and give students the opportunity to acquire materials for it

Activity #1
Quiz - Distribute quizzes for chapters 3-4 and give students about 10 minutes to complete them.

(NOTE: The quizzes may either be the short answer study guides or the multiple choice version.) Have students exchange papers. Grade the quizzes as a class. Collect the papers for recording the grades. (If you used the multiple choice version as a quiz, take a few minutes to discuss the answers for the short answer version if your students are using the short answer version for their study guides.)

Activity #2
Take students to the library/media center. Distribute the Nonfiction Reading Assignment Sheet and discuss it with students. After reading the PROMPT section, have students brainstorm more of our "fighters" and use that list to assign specific students to research specific biographies. Give students time in the library to get reading materials.

Activity #3
Tell students that prior to your next class meeting they need to have completed the prereading and reading work for chapters 5-6.

NONFICTION READING ASSIGNMENT - *Wrinkle in Time*

PROMPT

Coming up in Chapter 5 is this passage:

"All through the universe it's being fought [the battle against Evil, all through the cosmos, and my, but it's a grand and exciting battle. . . . some of our best fighters have come right from your own planet, and it's a *little* planet, dears, out on the edge of a little galaxy. You can be proud that it's done so well."

"Who have our fighters been?" Calvin asked. . . . "Leonardo da Vinci?" Calvin suggested tentatively, "And Michelangelo?"

"And Shakespeare," Charles Wallace called out, "and Bach! And Pasteur and Madame Curie and Einstein!"

Now Calvin's voice rang with confidence. "And Schweitzer and Gandhi and Buddha and Beethoven and Rembrandt and St. Francis!" "Now you, Meg," Mrs. Whatsit ordered.

"Oh, Euclid, I suppose." Meg was in such an agony of impatience that her voice grated irritably. "And Copernicus. . . . . "

ASSIGNMENT

You are to research biographical information about the person to whom you will be assigned. Find out who the person was/is, when he/she lived, what his/her contributions were to the world, and all basic biographical information. Take notes and fill out a Nonfiction Reading Assignment Sheet for each nonfiction book or article you read relating to this assignment.

LESSON FIVE

Objectives
1. To review the main ideas and events in chapters 5-6
2. To preview and read chapters 7-10
3. To give students the opportunity to practice writing to inform
4. To give the teacher the opportunity to evaluate students' writing skills

Activity #1
Give students a few minutes to formulate answers for the study questions for chapters 5-6 and then discuss the students' answers in detail.

Activity #2
Tell students that prior to your next class period they should have done the prereading and reading work for chapters 7-10.

Activity #3
Distribute Writing Assignment #1. Discuss the directions in detail and give students ample time to complete the assignment. If students finish this assignment before the end of this class period, they may begin working on the prereading and reading assignment for chapters 7-10.

LESSONS SIX AND SEVEN

Objectives
1. To check students' research
2. To expose students to information about a wide variety of people who have made contributions to our society throughout history
3. To give students the opportunity to practice public speaking
4. To review the main ideas and events from chapters 7-10

Activity #1
Spend your class time listening to and discussing the biographical oral reports from individual students.

Activity #2
When the oral reports finish (probably sometime in Lesson Seven), give students a few minutes to formulate answers to the study questions for chapters 7-10 and discuss students' answers in detail.

WRITING ASSIGNMENT #1 - *A Wrinkle in Time*

PROMPT
You have researched biographical information about a famous person, and sometime in the next couple of class meetings you will have to give an oral report telling about that person. The purpose of this assignment is to help you prepare your oral presentation by writing out what you intend to say during your presentation.

PREWRITING
Much of your prewriting has been done through your research and note-taking. The biggest part of your prewriting will be to choose which facts you will present and to organize them. Look through all of your notes. Make marks to identify the parts you definitely want to use in your presentation. Then organize your notes in chronological order; that is the easiest and most logical way to present biographical information to an audience.

DRAFTING
Write a paragraph in which you introduce your person.

The paragraphs in the body of your composition should flow chronologically--perhaps one paragraph for the person's early life, middle years, and then later years and death. The last paragraph in the body of your composition should summarize your person's life's work--the contributions he/she has made.

The final paragraph of your composition should include your final remarks about the person whom you have researched.

PROMPT
When you finish the rough draft of your paper, ask a student who sits near you to read it. After reading your rough draft, he/she should tell you what he/she liked best about your work, which parts were difficult to understand, and ways in which your work could be improved. Reread your paper considering your critic's comments and make the corrections you think are necessary.

PROOFREADING
Do a final proofreading of your paper double-checking your grammar, spelling, organization, and the clarity of your ideas.

LESSON EIGHT

Objectives
1. To preview the study questions and vocabulary for chapters 11-12
2. To read chapters 11-12

Activity
Tell students that prior to your next class period they should have completed the prereading and reading work for chapters 11-12. Give students this class period to work on this assignment silently.

LESSONS NINE AND TEN

Objectives
1. To review the main ideas and events from chapters 11-12
2. To prepare students to discuss *A Wrinkle in Time* on interpretive and critical levels
2. To begin discussing *A Wrinkle in Time* on interpretive and critical levels

Activity #1
Give students a few minutes to formulate answers to the study questions for chapters 11-12 and then discuss students' answers in detail.

Activity #2
Choose the questions from the Extra Discussion Questions/Writing Assignments which seem most appropriate for your students. A class discussion of these questions is most effective if students have been given the opportunity to formulate answers to the questions prior to the discussion. To this end, you may either have all the students formulate answers to all the questions, divide your class into groups and assign one or more questions to each group, or assign one question to each student in your class. The option you choose will make a difference in the amount of class time needed for this activity. Two class periods are allotted assuming you will cover most of the questions offered. If you need less time, skip to Lesson Eleven.

Activity #3
After students have had ample time to formulate answers to the questions, begin your class discussion of the questions and the ideas presented by the questions. Be sure students take notes during the discussion so they have information to study for the unit test.

EXTRA WRITING ASSIGNMENTS AND/OR DISCUSSION QUESTIONS
A Wrinkle in Time

<u>Interpretation</u>

1. Where is the climax of the story?
2. How does Meg change from the beginning to the end of the story?
3. Explain the use of setting in *A Wrinkle in Time*.
4. Does Ms. L'Engle attempt to make the story believable? Why or why not?
5. Define "fantasy," "fairy tale," "fable," "myth," and "science fiction" and explain which terms relate to this story.

<u>Critical</u>

6. There are many references to glasses and sight in the novel. Use several of them to explain the author's point about sight versus understanding.
7. Explain the purpose or use of each character in the story.
8. Explain how the title of the book is appropriate.
9. Explain how things aren't always what they seem to be in the story.
10. Characterize Madeleine L'Engle's style of writing. How does it contribute to the value of the novel?
11. According to the author, is it better to be like everyone else or to be an individual? Defend your answer using examples from the text.
12. How does *The Tempest* relate to *A Wrinkle in Time*?
13. In our society we often differentiate between the "arts" and the "sciences" almost to the point of making them opposites of each other. Madeleine L'Engle recognizes their differences yet shows how they can complement one another for a larger purpose. Explain how this is shown in *A Wrinkle in Time*.
14. What faults in our society does Madeleine L'Engle point out in *A Wrinkle in Time*?
15. Explain the use of light and dark imagery in the story using examples from the text.
16. A few times there are references made to the saying "laughing in the dark." What does that saying mean, and how may it relate to the story?
17. Compare and contrast the beings on Uriel, Camazotz, and Ixchel with humans on Earth.
18. One of the main themes in the novel relates to communications. Explain all the ways of communication shown in the novel.
19. Mrs. Murry speaks of a "willing suspension of disbelief." What is that? Why do we need to have a willing suspension of disbelief as we read this story?
20. "Like and equal are two entirely different things." Explain what that means and how it relates to the story.
21. In chapter 3, Mrs. Murry says she read to Charles Wallace from Genesis. What relevance does that have to the story?
22. Explain the role of religion in *A Wrinkle in Time*.

Wrinkle Extra Discussion Questions page 2

Personal Response
23. What were we supposed to learn from reading *A Wrinkle in Time*?
24. Did you enjoy reading this story? Why or why not?
25. Explain the difference between doing well in school and being "educated."
26. Do you like reading science fiction/science fantasy stories? Why or why not?
27. Where would you go if you could tesser?

LESSON ELEVEN

Objective
> To review all of the vocabulary work done in this unit

Activity
> Choose one (or more) of the vocabulary review activities listed on the next page(s) and spend your class period as directed in the activity. Some of the materials for these review activities are located in the Extra Activities section in this unit.

VOCABULARY REVIEW ACTIVITIES

1. Divide your class into two teams and have an old-fashioned spelling or definition bee.

2. Give each of your students (or students in groups of two, three or four) a *Wrinkle in Time* Vocabulary Word Search Puzzle. The person (group) to find all of the vocabulary words in the puzzle first wins.

3. Give students a *Wrinkle in Time* Vocabulary Word Search Puzzle without the word list. The person or group to find the most vocabulary words in the puzzle wins.

4. Use a *Wrinkle in Time* Vocabulary Crossword Puzzle. Put the puzzle onto a transparency on the overhead projector (so everyone can see it), and do the puzzle together as a class.

5. Give students a *Wrinkle in Time* Vocabulary Matching Worksheet to do.

6. Divide your class into two teams. Use *A Wrinkle in Time* vocabulary words with their letters jumbled as a word list. Student 1 from Team A faces off against Student 1 from Team B. You write the first jumbled word on the board. The first student (1A or 1B) to unscramble the word wins the chance for his/her team to score points. If 1A wins the jumble, go to student 2A and give him/her a definition. He/she must give you the correct spelling of the vocabulary word which fits that definition. If he/she does, Team A scores a point, and you give student 3A a definition for which you expect a correctly spelled matching vocabulary word. Continue giving Team A definitions until some team member makes an incorrect response. An incorrect response sends the game back to the jumbled-word face off, this time with students 2A and 2B. Instead of repeating giving definitions to the first few students of each team, continue with the student after the one who gave the last incorrect response on the team. For example, if Team B wins the jumbled-word face-off, and student 5B gave the last incorrect answer for Team B, you would start this round of definition questions with student 6B, and so on. The team with the most points wins!

7. Have students write a story in which they correctly use as many vocabulary words as possible. Have students read their compositions orally! Post the most original compositions on your bulletin board.

LESSON TWELVE

Objectives
    1. To review and reinforce the main ideas and events of the story
    2. To consider the significance of several of the quotations from the story
    3. To take a closer look at the importance of the language selected in writing the story

Activity #1

    Distribute the Quotations Worksheet. Discuss the significance or importance of each quote listed.

LESSONS THIRTEEN AND FOURTEEN

Objectives
    1. To give students the opportunity to be creative and use their imaginations
    2. To give students the opportunity to work together in small groups
    3. To spin-off on the idea of alien worlds presented in the novel

Activity #1

    Have your students (as an entire class) describe the earth as a world, a planet different from others. As they do so, write down the characteristics on the board. From these characteristics, make a list of the *kinds* of things students used to describe their world.

Activity #2

    Divide your class into small groups (about three students per group). Explain to the groups that their assignment is to create an alien world. It may have any kind of physical characteristics and inhabitants that the students want to make it have. They should make their plans for their worlds as detailed as possible using the list of kinds of characteristics they used to describe the earth as a guide. All students in the group should jot down the characteristics of their world to use as a guide for the writing assignment which will follow.

    You may wish to offer a prize to the group that creates the most interesting alien world. In the writing assignment which follows, students create brochures for their worlds, persuading travelers to visit their worlds. Later, students will exchange and read all of the brochures. One way to determine the "winner" would be to take a vote to see how many students would visit each alien world. The world with the most would-be visitors would win!

QUOTATIONS WORKSHEET - *A Wrinkle in Time*

1. It was his mother's mind, and Meg's that he probed with frightening accuracy.(1)

2. You're much too straightforward to be able to pretend to be what you aren't. (1)

3. Tell your sister I'm all right. . . . Tell her my intentions are good. (1)

4. You don't have to take everything so personally. Use a happy medium, for heaven's sake. (2)

5. I think it will be better if people go on thinking I'm not very bright. They won't hate me so much. (2)

6. Mother's all right. She's not one of us. But she's all right. . . . What do you mean, one of us? Meg demanded. (2)

7. Meg has it tough . . . she's not really one thing or another. (2)

8. French. Pascal. The heart has its reasons, whereof reason knows nothing. (2)

9. Nothing deters a good man from doing what is honorable. (2)

10. I love them all, and they don't give a hoot about me. . . . You don't know how lucky you are to be loved. (3)

11. Are there any more morons like Meg and Charles around? . . . If so, I should meet more of them. (3)

12. I feel as though I were just being born! I'm not alone any more! Do you realize what that means to me? (3)

Wrinkle Quotations Worksheet Page 2

13. But you see, Meg, just because we don't understand doesn't mean that the explanation doesn't exist. (3)

14. Charles Wallace's difference isn't physical. It's in essence. Meg sighed heavily, took off her glasses and twirled them, put them back on again. (3)

15. Nothing is hopeless; we must hope for everything. (4)

16. The more a man knows, the less he talks. (4)

17. The work proves the craftsman. (4)

18. Meg's eyes ached from the strain of looking and seeing nothing. (4)

19. Experience is the mother of knowledge. (5)

20. We are such stuff as dreams are made of. (5)

21. How small is the earth to him who looks from heaven. (5)

22. And the light shineth in the darkness; and the darkness comprehended it not. (5)

23. I do not know everything; still many things I understand. (6)

24. Only a fool is not afraid. (6)

25. I have been waiting for you, my dears, the man said. His voice was kind and gentle, not at all the cold and frightening voice Meg had expected. (7)

Wrinkle Quotations Worksheet Page 3

26. . . . after all you are very young and very impressionable, and the younger the better, my little man. The younger the better. (7)

27. Murder is a most primitive word. . . . There is no such thing as murder on Camazotz. IT takes care of all such things. (8)

28. Maybe I don't like being different, . . . but I don't want to be like everybody else, either. (8)

29. Red fog glazed her eyes. (9)

30. Time is different on Camazotz. Our time, inadequate though it is, at least is straightforward. (10)

31. You're supposed to be able to help! (10)

32. Then you're feeling again. . . . I'm afraid it is going to hurt, Meg. (10)

33. . . . the earth's my home, and I'd rather be there than anywhere else in the world--I mean, the universe-- and I can't wait to get back, but we make some awful bloopers there. (11)

34. It must be a very limiting thing, this seeing. (11)

LESSONS FIFTEEN AND SIXTEEN

Objectives
1. To give students the opportunity to practice writing to persuade
2. To evaluate students' group work
3. To give the teacher a chance to evaluate students' writing skills

Activity
Distribute Writing Assignment #2. Discuss the directions orally in detail. Give students ample time to complete this assignment.

NOTE: Two class periods are allowed for this activity: one for deciding what should go in the brochure and to create a general layout, and the second for actually writing the copy and putting it together. Length of time needed will vary depending on the ability and interest levels of your students.

Also, it will help students if you have a variety of travel brochures available for them to look at as they do this assignment. See your local travel agent for some free samples.

LESSON SEVENTEEN

Objectives
1. To let students share and enjoy each other's work
2. To bring the group activity to a close

Activity
Let students have this class time to read each other's brochures. If you are having a contest, use the end of this class period to vote on which group created the most enticing alien world!

LESSON EIGHTEEN

Objectives
1. To give students the opportunity to practice writing their personal opinions
2. To give the teacher the opportunity to evaluate students' writing skills

Activity
Distribute Writing Assignment #3. Discuss the directions in detail and give students ample time to complete the assignment.

While students are working on this assignment, call individual students to your desk or some other private area for individual writing conferences based on the first two writing assignments. An evaluation form is enclosed for your convenience.

WRITING ASSIGNMENT #2 - *A Wrinkle in Time*

PROMPT

Have you ever been sitting at home watching television and during a commercial break seen an advertisement come on for a cruise to some exotic land or a terrific vacation spot? Those ads look great! We just want to pack our bags and get there as soon as possible! Guess what? We're victims of persuasion.

You have created an alien world. Now you need to get some of those tourists' dollars into your alien economy. So, it is your job to create a brochure persuading people to come to your alien world. You will have this class period and one more to complete this assignment.

PREWRITING

Look over your notes describing your alien world. What things will attract the most people? Those are the things you emphasize in your brochure. Make a list of things you want to include in your brochure. After you decide what will go in your brochure, you need to decide *how* it will go in. Make a layout; design your brochure. What size will it be? Will there be any pictures or graphics? Will it be stapled, folded or left flat? Will it be hand written or typed--or done on a computer? Plan out all the details.

DRAFTING

Once you know what you're going to put in and how you want it to look, you need to *do it*. Divide up the work. Assign copy writing to one or two group members and the artwork (if there is any) to another group member. Make a rough draft, look at it objectively, and decide if you want (or need) to change anything. Then make a final copy.

PROMPT

When you finish the rough draft of your brochure, ask a student who sits near you to read it. After reading your rough draft, he/she should tell you what he/she liked best about your work, which parts were difficult to understand, and ways in which your work could be improved. Reread your brochure considering your critic's comments and make the corrections you think are necessary.

PROOFREADING

Do a final proofreading of your brochure double-checking your grammar, spelling, organization, and the clarity of your ideas.

WRITING ASSIGNMENT #3 - *A Wrinkle in Time*

PROMPT
There are a number of ideas that are touched upon in this story, and we simply don't have enough time to delve into them all in detail. So your assignment is to consider each of the quotations from the quotations worksheet, choose one about which you have some opinions, and write a composition in which you give your own opinions about the topic or idea the quotation suggests.

PREWRITING
Read through all of the quotations again. Is there one that pops out at you for some reason? Maybe there is one quote that you can relate to more than the others. Think about the quotes and choose one about which to write.

Write out the quote at the top of a scratch sheet of paper. Under it jot down notes, ideas, impressions the quote brings to your mind. When you have finished brainstorming, look at the notes you have jotted down. You won't use every idea you've thought about, but looking at your ideas should give you some sparks to help you get started.

Make a little outline of your ideas and shuffle them until you come up with an arrangement that flows nicely and is logical.

DRAFTING
The organization and drafting of this composition is pretty flexible because of the nature of the assignment. You should have a definite introduction, a body to your composition, and a closing. Remember the fundamentals of writing.

PROMPT
When you finish the rough draft of your composition, ask a student who sits near you to read it. After reading your rough draft, he/she should tell you what he/she liked best about your work, which parts were difficult to understand, and ways in which your work could be improved. Reread your paper considering your critic's comments and make the corrections you think are necessary.

PROOFREADING
Do a final proofreading of your composition double-checking your grammar, spelling, organization, and the clarity of your ideas.

WRITING EVALUATION FORM - *A Wrinkle in Time*

Name _____ Date _____

Grade _____

Circle One For Each Item:

Grammar:	excellent	good	fair	poor
Spelling:	excellent	good	fair	poor
Punctuation:	excellent	good	fair	poor
Legibility:	excellent	good	fair	poor

Strengths:

Weaknesses:

Comments/Suggestions:

LESSON NINETEEN

Objective
> To review the main ideas presented in *A Wrinkle in Time*

Activity #1
> Choose one of the review games/activities included in this guide and spend your class period as outlined there. Some materials for these activities are located in the Extra Activities section of this unit.

Activity #2
> Remind students that the Unit Test will be in the next class meeting. Stress the review of the Study Guides and their class notes as a last-minute, brush-up review for homework.

REVIEW GAMES/ACTIVITIES - *A Wrinkle in Time*

1. Ask the class to make up a unit test for *A Wrinkle in Time*. The test should have 4 sections: matching, true/false, short answer, and essay. Students may use 1/2 period to make the test and then swap papers and use the other 1/2 class period to take a test a classmate has devised. (open book) You may want to use the unit test included in this guide or take questions from the students' unit tests to formulate your own test.

2. Take 1/2 period for students to make up true and false questions (including the answers). Collect the papers and divide the class into two teams. Draw a big tic-tac-toe board on the board. Make one team X and one team O. Ask questions to each side, giving each student one turn. If the question is answered correctly, that students' team's letter (X or O) is placed in the box. If the answer is incorrect, no mark is placed in the box. The object is to get three marks in a row like tic-tac-toe. You may want to keep track of the number of games won for each team.

3. Take 1/2 period for students to make up questions (true/false and short answer). Collect the questions. Divide the class into two teams. You'll alternate asking questions to individual members of teams A & B (like in a spelling bee). The question keeps going from A to B until it is correctly answered, then a new question is asked. A correct answer does not allow the team to get another question. Correct answers are +2 points; incorrect answers are -1 point.

4. Have students pair up and quiz each other from their study guides and class notes.

5. Give students a *Wrinkle in Time* crossword puzzle to complete.

6. Divide your class into two teams. Use *A Wrinkle in Time* crossword words with their letters jumbled as a word list. Student 1 from Team A faces off against Student 1 from Team B. You write the first jumbled word on the board. The first student (1A or 1B) to unscramble the word wins the chance for his/her team to score points. If 1A wins the jumble, go to student 2A and give him/her a clue. He/she must give you the correct word which matches that clue. If he/she does, Team A scores a point, and you give student 3A a clue for which you expect another correct response. Continue giving Team A clues until some team member makes an incorrect response. An incorrect response sends the game back to the jumbled-word face off, this time with students 2A and 2B. Instead of repeating giving clues to the first few students of each team, continue with the student after the one who gave the last incorrect response on the team. For example, if Team B wins the jumbled-word face-off, and student 5B gave the last incorrect answer for Team B, you would start this round of clue questions with student 6B, and so on. The team with the most points wins!

UNIT TESTS

SHORT ANSWER UNIT TEST 1 - A Wrinkle in Time

I. Matching

___ 1. MORON   A. Author

___ 2. WHICH   B. A most primitive word; kill

___ 3. CALVIN   C. Place where IT has won

___ 4. LENGLE   D. Color of Calvin's hair

___ 5. ORANGE   E. The Happy ___ showed the children Earth surrounded by the Black Thing

___ 6. GLASSES   F. Meg's brother: ___ Wallace

___ 7. LIKE   G. Calvin called Charles a ___

___ 8. FEAR   H. Boy who went with Meg and Charles Wallace

___ 9. MEDIUM   I. Planet where they rested

___10. IMPATIENCE   J. Gives Meg her love

___11. CAMAZOTZ   K. ___ and equal are not the same

___12. CHARLES   L. One of Meg's faults

___13. URIEL   M. The ___ Mrs. W gave Meg allowed her to get in to see her father

___14. MURDER   N. Feeling towards the Dark Thing

Wrinkle Short Answer Unit Test 1 Page 2

II. Short Answer

1. Why didn't Mrs. Murry worry about the children?

2. Who is the Happy Medium?

3. What were the people on Camazotz like?

4. What did Mrs. Who's spectacles do for Meg?

5. What is IT?

6. Why is Meg the only one who can get Charles Wallace?

7. To what does Mrs. Whatsit compare human lives?

8. What did Meg have that IT did not?

Wrinkle Short Answer Unit Test 1 Page 3

III. Quotes - Explain 10 of the following quotes:

1. I think it will be better if people go on thinking I'm not very bright. They won't hate me so much. (2)

2. I love them all, and they don't give a hoot about me. . . . You don't know how lucky you are to be loved. (3)

3. I do not know everything; still many things I understand. (6)

4. Only a fool is not afraid. (6)

5. I have been waiting for you, my dears, the man said. His voice was kind and gentle, not at all the cold and frightening voice Meg had expected. (7)

6. . . . after all you are very young and very impressionable, and the younger the better, my little   man. The younger the better. (7)

7. Maybe I don't like being different, . . . but I don't want to be like everybody else, either. (8)

8. You're supposed to be able to help! (10)

9. Then you're feeling again. . . . I'm afraid it is going to hurt, Meg. (10)

10. . . . the earth's my home, and I'd rather be there than anywhere else in the world--I mean, the universe-- and I can't wait to get back, but we make some awful bloopers there. (11)

11. It must be a very limiting thing, this seeing. (11)

Wrinkle Short Answer Unit Test Page 4

III. Vocabulary

Listen to the words given. Write them down. Go back later and write in the definitions.

1.

2.

3.

4.

5.

6.

7.

8.

9.

10.

SHORT ANSWER UNIT TEST 2 - A Wrinkle in Time

I. Matching

___ 1. MEDIUM   A. Meg's Ixchel friend: Aunt ___

___ 2. BUNCOMBE   B. She saved Charles Wallce

___ 3. ATOMS   C. Short-cut or wrinkle

___ 4. RHYTHM   D. Meg's family name

___ 5. LENGLE   E. First book of the Bible

___ 6. FEAR   F. Small particles

___ 7. MEGAPARSEC   G. The Happy ___ showed the children Earth surrounded by the Black Thing

___ 8. TESSERACT   H. Everything on Camazotz moved in perfect ___

___ 9. IMPATIENCE   I. Feeling towards the Dark Thing

___ 10. BEAST   J. The _____ of 4 is 2: ___ root

___ 11. GENESIS   K. Author

___ 12. MURRY   L. Meg's nickname referring to 3.26 million light years

___ 13. MEG   M. Mrs. Whatsit stole her sheets

___ 14. SQUARE   N. One of Meg's faults

Wrinkle Short Answer Unit Test 2 Page 2

II. Short Answer

1. Why does Calvin call Charles a moron?

2. What is the rumor about Mr. Murry? What is the truth?

3. Why won't Mrs. Murry be worried about Meg and Charles Wallace?

4. What happens when a star dies in battle with the Black Thing?

5. Why is the danger greatest for Charles Wallace?

6. What were the people of Camazotz like?

7. Why does Charles Wallace finally allow himself to be hypnotized?

Wrinkle Short Answer Unit Test 2 Page 3

8. What is IT?

9. What are the creatures on Ixchel like?

10. Why is Meg the only one who can go to save Charles Wallace?

11. To what does Mrs. Whatsit compare human lives?

12. What did Meg do to get Charles Wallace away from IT?

rinkle Short Answer Unit Test 2 Page 4

III. Composition

Explain two of the themes or ideas presented by Madeleine L'Engle in *A Wrinkle in Time*. Write one complete paragraph for each of the two themes you choose.

IV. Vocabulary - Listen to the words and write them down. Go back later and write the correct definitions next to the words.

1.
2.
3.
4.
5.
6.
7.
8.
9.
10.

KEY: SHORT ANSWER UNIT TESTS - *A Wrinkle in Time*

The short answer questions are taken directly from the study guides.
If you need to look up the answers, you will find them in the study guide section.

Answers to the composition questions will vary depending on your
class discussions and the level of your students.

For the vocabulary section of the test, choose ten of the words
from the vocabulary lists to read orally for your students.

The answers to the matching section of the test are below.

Answers to the matching section of the Advanced Short Answer Unit Test
are the same as for Short Answer Unit Test #2.

Test #1	**Test #2**
1. G	1. G
2. J	2. M
3. H	3. F
4. A	4. H
5. D	5. K
6. M	6. I
7. K	7. L
8. N	8. C
9. E	9. N
10. L	10. A
11. C	11. E
12. F	12. D
13. I	13. B
14. B	14. J

ADVANCED SHORT ANSWER UNIT TEST - A Wrinkle in Time

I. Matching

___ 1. MEDIUM   A. Meg's Ixchel friend: Aunt ___

___ 2. BUNCOMBE   B. She saved Charles Wallce

___ 3. ATOMS   C. Short-cut or wrinkle

___ 4. RHYTHM   D. Meg's family name

___ 5. LENGLE   E. First book of the Bible

___ 6. FEAR   F. Small particles

___ 7. MEGAPARSEC   G. The Happy ___ showed the children Earth surrounded by the Black Thing

___ 8. TESSERACT   H. Everything on Camazotz moved in perfect ___

___ 9. IMPATIENCE   I. Feeling towards the Dark Thing

___ 10. BEAST   J. The _____ of 4 is 2: ___ root

___ 11. GENESIS   K. Author

___ 12. MURRY   L. Meg's nickname referring to 3.26 million light years

___ 13. MEG   M. Mrs. Whatsit stole her sheets

___ 14. SQUARE   N. One of Meg's faults

Wrinkle Advanced Short Answer Unit Test Page 2

1. Explain how things aren't always what they seem to be in the

2. What faults in our society does Madeleine L'Engle point out in *A Wrinkle in Time*?

3. Compare and contrast the beings on Uriel, Camazotz, and Ixchel with humans on Earth.

4. One of the main themes in the novel relates to communications. Explain all the ways of communication shown in the novel.

5. In chapter 3, Mrs. Murry says she read to Charles Wallace from Genesis. What relevance does that have to the story?

Wrinkle Advanced Short Answer Unit Test Page 3

IV. Composition

About *A Wrinkle in Time*, the Saturday Review said, "It has the general appearance of being science fiction, but it is not. . . . There is mystery, mysticism, a feeling of indefinable, brooding horror . . . The pervading theme is love . . . One feels that this book quests desperately for something it never touches. It is original, different, exciting." Defend this statement using examples from the book.

Wrinkle Advanced Short Answer Unit Test Page 4

IV. Vocabulary - Listen to the words and write them down. Go back later and write a paragraph using all of the words. The paragraph must relate in some way to *A Wrinkle in Time*.

MULTIPE CHOICE UNIT TEST 1 - A Wrinkle in Time

I. Matching

___ 1. ORANGE   A. The man on the chair wanted to ___ the children

___ 2. SONNET   B. She saved Charles Wallce

___ 3. GLASSES   C. She did confine thee into a ____ Pine

___ 4. CLOVEN   D. Mrs. Whatsit compares human lives to a ____

___ 5. LENGLE   E. Meg's brother: ___ Wallace

___ 6. RHYTHM   F. ____ and equal are not the same

___ 7. HYPNOTIZE   G. The ___ Mrs. W gave Meg allowed her to get in to see her father

___ 8. CHARLES   H. Author

___ 9. CALVIN   I. Color of Calvin's hair

___10. LIKE   J. Feeling towards the Dark Thing

___11. IXCHEL   K. It

___12. MEG   L. Everything on Camazotz moved in perfect ___

___13. FEAR   M. The creatures at this place are kind, gentle beings

___14. EVIL   N. Boy who went with Meg and Charles Wallace

Wrinkle Multiple Choice Unit Test 1 Page 2

II. Multiple Choice

1. What did Mrs. Whatsit do that made Charles Wallace scold her?
    a. She insulted his mother.
    b. She stole Mrs. Buncombe's sheets.
    c. She interrupted him.
    d. She called him a moron.

2. Why does Calvin call Charles a moron?
    a. He is angry at Charles Wallace.
    b. Charles Wallace is not very bright.
    c. He was preconditioned in the concept of his mentality.
    d. He was trying to make himself look more important.

3. How does Calvin feel about his family?
    a. He loves them but thinks they don't care for him.
    b. He doesn't care for them.
    c. He thinks they're all crazy.
    d. He thinks they're all morons.

4. What does Mrs. Murry say is Charles Wallace's difference?
    a. He is far more intelligent than most other people on Earth.
    b. He is different in essence, not physically.
    c. He is telepathic.
    d. He is more sensitive and has an overactive imagination.

5. What is the rumor about Mr. Murry?
    a. He was killed in a government scientific experiment.
    b. He was picked up by aliens.
    c. He was severely mutilated in a science experiment.
    d. He has gone off with another woman.

6. For what were the "flowers" used?
    a. To help the humans breathe
    b. As a sleeping potion
    c. As food
    d. To help them tesser

Wrinkle Multiple Choice Unit Test 1 Page 3

7. Why won't Mrs. Murry be worried about Meg and Charles Wallace?
   a. She thinks they've gone to a movie.
   b. She knows they won't get into trouble.
   c. She trusts the Mrs. W's.
   d. She'll think they've only been gone five minutes.

8. How was Camazotz different from Earth?
   a. It was much prettier.
   b. All the people did the same things at the same time in the same way.
   c. The people used flowers to help them breathe.
   d. It was dark; there was no sunlight.

9. Why is the danger greatest for Charles Wallace?
   a. He is the youngest and most vulnerable.
   b. He is the smartest.
   c. He is the smallest.
   d. His special mind reading skills put him at risk.

10. Why does Charles Wallace finally allow himself to be hypnotized?
    a. It was the only way to find his father.
    b. He thought he could get out of the hypnosis whenever he wanted.
    c. He was tricked into it.
    d. Meg asked him to.

11. What is IT?
    a. Big pulsating brain that controls everything that succumbs to it
    b. A government experiment gone wrong
    c. God
    d. Mr. Murry

12. How did Meg use her faults?
    a. She became stubborn and refused to succumb to IT.
    b. She chattered incessantly to avoid IT.
    c. She got angry and punched IT in the face.
    d. She became impatient and punched IT in the face.

13. How did Meg get in to see her father?
    a. She bribed IT.
    b. She thought the right thoughts.
    c. She broke in.
    d. She used the glasses Mrs. W. gave her.

Wrinkle Multiple Choice Unit Test 1 Page 4

14. How did Mr. Murry get Calvin, Meg, and himself out of IT's domain?
    a. They used a secret passage he remembered.
    b. He and the children tessered.
    c. They used Mrs. W's glasses.
    d. They thought themselves out of it.

15. Why is Meg angry at her father?
    a. He broke her glasses.
    b. He never explained why he left home.
    c. He left Calvin behind.
    d. She blames him for messing up and sending them to a strange planet.

16. What are the creatures on Ixchel like?
    a. They are small ITs.
    b. They've been taken over by the Black Thing.
    c. They are kind and gentle.
    d. They are distant and suspicious.

17. Why is Meg the only one who can go to save Charles Wallace?
    a. Only she knows the way.
    b. She understands him the best.
    c. The glasses will only work for her.
    d. IT won't suspect her.

18. To what does Mrs. Whatsit compare human lives?
    a. A sonnet
    b. A song
    c. A bird
    d. Morning light

19. What did Meg use to get Charles Wallace away from IT?
    a. Light
    b. Poetry
    c. Mathematics
    d. Love

Wrinkle Multiple Choice Unit Test 1 Page 5

III. Vocabulary   Match the definitions to the appropriate words.

____ 1. FURY   A. Small

____ 2. CONFIDINGLY   B. Tranquility

____ 3. DISSOLUTION   C. Put off to a later time

____ 4. SIMULTANEOUSLY   D. Sharp; severe

____ 5. ASSUAGED   E. Short-lived; lasting only a short time

____ 6. ACUTE   F. Rage; violent anger

____ 7. METAMORPHOSE   G. Spiteful; malicious

____ 8. ANGUISH   H. Change in form; transform

____ 9. BLISS   I. Excessive or uncontrollable fear or other emotions

____ 10. PUNY   J. Agonizing physical or mental pain

____ 11. VICIOUS   K. Became less dense by scattering; dispelled

____ 12. INADVERTENTLY   L. Backward flow of air, as from a propeller

____ 13. SERENITY   M. Unintentionally; by accident

____ 14. SUBSIDED   N. Decomposition into fragments or parts

____ 15. UNOBSCURED   O. Abated; settled down; lessened

____ 16. EPHEMERAL   P. Made less severe

____ 17. DEFER   Q. Not obstructed; in full view

____ 18. DISPERSED   R. At the same time

____ 19. BACKWASH   S. Serene happiness

____ 20. HYSTERIA   T. Comfortingly; seeking or giving in confidence

Wrinkle Multiple Choice Unit Test 1 Page 6

IV. Composition

      Choose two of the main conflicts in the story and explain them as they relate to the story. Also tell if they are resolved or not. Write at least one complete paragraph for each of the conflicts you choose.

MULTIPLE CHOICE UNIT TEST 2 - A Wrinkle in Time

I. Matching

___ 1. DENNYS   A. Meg's brother: ___ Wallace

___ 2. MURRY   B. Meg's family name

___ 3. CHARLES   C. First book of the Bible

___ 4. FEAR   D. Gives Meg her love

___ 5. DARK   E. She did confine thee into a ____ Pine

___ 6. GENESIS   F. A twin

___ 7. MORON   G. Feeling towards the Dark Thing

___ 8. CLOVEN   H. Meg's Ixchel friend: Aunt ___

___ 9. STAR   I. Calvin called Charles a ___

___ 10. MEGAPARSEC   J. Meg's nickname referring to 3.26 million light years

___ 11. WHICH   K. Planet where they rested

___ 12. URIEL   L. Laughing in the _____

___ 13. MURDER   M. A most primitive word; kill

___ 14. BEAST   N. When a ___ dies in battle with the Black Thing, it becomes a person like Mrs. Whatsit

Wrinkle Multiple Choice Unit Test 2 Page 2

II. Multiple Choice

1. What did Mrs. Whatsit do that made Charles Wallace scold her?
    a. She called him a moron.
    b. She insulted his mother.
    c. She interrupted him.
    d. She stole Mrs. Buncombe's sheets.

2. Why does Calvin call Charles a moron?
    a. He was trying to make himself look more important.
    b. He was preconditioned in the concept of his mentality.
    c. He is angry at Charles Wallace.
    d. Charles Wallace is not very bright.

3. How does Calvin feel about his family?
    a. He doesn't care for them.
    b. He thinks they're all crazy.
    c. He thinks they're all morons.
    d. He loves them but thinks they don't care for him.

4. What does Mrs. Murry say is Charles Wallace's difference?
    a. He is telepathic.
    b. He is far more intelligent than most other people on Earth.
    c. He is different in essence, not physically.
    d. He is more sensitive and has an overactive imagination.

5. What is the rumor about Mr. Murry?
    a. He has gone off with another woman.
    b. He was killed in a government scientific experiment.
    c. He was severely mutilated in a science experiment.
    d. He was picked up by aliens.

6. For what were the "flowers" used?
    a. To help them tesser
    b. To help the humans breathe
    c. As food
    d. As a sleeping potion

Wrinkle Multiple Choice Unit Test 2 Page 3

7. Why won't Mrs. Murry be worried about Meg and Charles Wallace?
    a. She trusts the Mrs. W's.
    b. She knows they won't get into trouble.
    c. She'll think they've only been gone five minutes.
    d. She thinks they've gone to a movie.

8. How was Camazotz different from Earth?
    a. It was dark; there was no sunlight.
    b. The people used flowers to help them breathe.
    c. It was much prettier.
    d. All the people did the same things at the same time in the same way.

9. Why is the danger greatest for Charles Wallace?
    a. His special mind reading skills put him at risk.
    b. He is the youngest and most vulnerable.
    c. He is the smallest.
    d. He is the smartest.

10. Why does Charles Wallace finally allow himself to be hypnotized?
    a. He thought he could get out of the hypnosis whenever he wanted.
    b. Meg asked him to.
    c. He was tricked into it.
    d. It was the only way to find his father.

11. What is IT?
    a. A government experiment gone wrong
    b. God
    c. Big pulsating brain that controls everything that succumbs to it
    d. Mr. Murry

12. How did Meg use her faults?
    a. She got angry and punched IT in the face.
    b. She chattered incessantly to avoid IT.
    c. She became impatient and punched IT in the face.
    d. She became stubborn and refused to succumb to IT.

13. How did Meg get in to see her father?
    a. She used the glasses Mrs. W. gave her.
    b. She broke in.
    c. She thought the right thoughts.
    d. She bribed IT

Wrinkle Multiple Choice Unit Test 2 Page 4

14. How did Mr. Murry get Calvin, Meg, and himself out of IT's domain?
   a. They used Mrs. W's glasses.
   b. They used a secret passage he remembered.
   c. He and the children tessered.
   d. They thought themselves out of it.

15. Why is Meg angry at her father?
   a. He broke her glasses.
   b. She blames him for messing up and sending them to a strange planet.
   c. He left Calvin behind.
   d. He never explained why he left home.

16. What are the creatures on Ixchel like?
   a. They are kind and gentle.
   b. They are distant and suspicious.
   c. They are small ITs.
   d. They've been taken over by the Black Thing.

17. Why is Meg the only one who can go to save Charles Wallace?
   a. The glasses will only work for her.
   b. Only she knows the way.
   c. She understands him the best.
   d. IT won't suspect her.

18. To what does Mrs. Whatsit compare human lives?
   a. A bird
   b. A song
   c. Morning light
   d. A sonnet

19. What did Meg use to get Charles Wallace away from IT?
   a. Poetry
   b. Love
   c. Mathematics
   d. Light

Wrinkle Multiple Choice Unit Test 2 Page 5

III. Vocabulary   Match the definitions to the appropriate words.

_____ 1. ACUTE   A. Ridiculous

_____ 2. INTOLERABLE   B. Not diluted; pure

_____ 3. DECIPHER   C. All powerful

_____ 4. EMANATED   D. Presenting favorable circumstances

_____ 5. BACKWASH   E. Abated; settled down; lessened

_____ 6. GESTURE   F. Sharp; severe

_____ 7. FURY   G. Wipe out; totally destroy

_____ 8. PUNY   H. Originated; came from

_____ 9. SIMULTANEOUSLY   I. Excessive or uncontrollable fear or other emotions

_____ 10. INDIGNATION   J. A motion of the limbs or body

_____ 11. SUBSIDED   K. At the same time

_____ 12. ASSIMILATE   L. To absorb or incorporate

_____ 13. ANNIHILATE   M. Backward flow of air, as from a propeller

_____ 14. OMNIPOTENT   N. Serene happiness

_____ 15. HYSTERIA   O. Small

_____ 16. ABSURD   P. Something that restores confidence

_____ 17. UNADULTERATED   Q. Anger aroused by something mean or unjust

_____ 18. PROPITIOUS   R. Rage; violent anger

_____ 19. REASSURANCE   S. Decode; to read or interpret

_____ 20. BLISS   T. Unbearable

ANSWER SHEET - MULTIPLE CHOICE TESTS
A Wrinkle in Time

I. Matching	II. Multiple Choice	IV. Vocabulary
1. ___	1. ___	1. ___
2. ___	2. ___	2. ___
3. ___	3. ___	3. ___
4. ___	4. ___	4. ___
5. ___	5. ___	5. ___
6. ___	6. ___	6. ___
7. ___	7. ___	7. ___
8. ___	8. ___	8. ___
9. ___	9. ___	9. ___
10. ___	10. ___	10. ___
11. ___	11. ___	11. ___
12. ___	12. ___	12. ___
13. ___	13. ___	13. ___
14. ___	14. ___	14. ___
	15. ___	15. ___
	16. ___	16. ___
	17. ___	17. ___
	18. ___	18. ___
	19. ___	19. ___
		20. ___

ANSWER KEY MULTIPLE CHOICE UNIT TESTS – *A Wrinkle in Time*

Answers to Unit Test 1 are in the left column. Answers to Unit Test 2 are in the right column.

I. Matching		II. Multiple Choice		IV. Vocabulary	
1. I	F	1. B	D	1. F	F
2. D	B	2. C	B	2. T	T
3. G	A	3. A	D	3. N	S
4. C	G	4. B	C	4. R	H
5. H	L	5. D	A	5. P	M
6. L	C	6. A	B	6. D	J
7. A	I	7. D	C	7. H	R
8. E	E	8. B	D	8. J	O
9. N	N	9. A	B	9. S	K
10. F	J	10. B	A	10. A	Q
11. M	D	11. A	C	11. G	E
12. B	K	12. A	D	12. M	L
13. J	M	13. D	A	13. B	G
14. K	H	14. B	C	14. O	C
		15. D	B	15. Q	I
		16. C	A	16. E	A
		17. B	C	17. C	B
		18. C	D	18. K	D
		19. D	B	19. L	P
				20. I	N

UNIT RESOURCE MATERIALS

BULLETIN BOARD IDEAS - *A Wrinkle in Time*

1. Save one corner of the board for the best of students' writing assignments.

2. In conjunction with Lesson One, Activity 1, have students bring in one article about a UFO sighting or any mysterious happening that cannot be explained by our current technology. (See Lesson One.) Use the time during Activity 1 for students to post their pictures on the board and explain what they represent.

3. Take one of the word search puzzles from the extra activities section, and with a marker copy it over in a large size on the bulletin board. Write the clue words to find to one side. Invite students prior to and after class to find the words and circle them on the bulletin board.

4. Title your board: BE AN INDIVIDUAL! Post pictures of people doing their own unique things--show them doing things different from "the crowd." Better yet, have students bring in pictures of themselves doing something they like to do and post those pictures on the board.

5. Make a bulletin board about space exploration and recent discoveries.

6. Post book "jackets" of other science fiction or science fantasy books students might enjoy reading.

7. Have students create pictures of the various worlds in *A Wrinkle in Time*. Laminate the best ones and keep them for next year's bulletin board.

8. Find or make a large picture of the Earth. Post it on the board and make a Dark Thing all around it. Make representations of the other worlds in the novel and put the Dark Thing around the appropriate worlds. Place something representative of the other worlds on them so they are recognizable. Make silhouettes of the children facing the worlds. Make representations of the three W's and place them on the board also.

9. Post articles about psychic or unexplainable events on the board.

10. Make a board about mythology.

11. Make a bulletin board about the "fighters" and post students' writing assignments next to the pictures of the "fighters" (Einstein, Beethoven, etc.).

EXTRA ACTIVITIES

One of the difficulties in teaching a novel is that all students don't read at the same speed. One student who likes to read may take the book home and finish it in a day or two. Sometimes a few students finish the in-class assignments early. The problem, then, is finding suitable extra activities for students.

The best thing I've found is to keep a little library in the classroom. For this unit on *A Wrinkle in Time*, you might check out from the school library other related books and articles about space exploration, myths and legends, the "fighters," and the author. Perhaps some students would like to read *The Tempest* or *Animal Farm* or some of Shakespeare's sonnets. If you like, you might include other science fiction or science fantasy books in your little library.

Other things you may keep on hand are puzzles. We have made some relating directly to *A Wrinkle in Time* for you. Feel free to duplicate them.

Some students may like to draw. You might devise a contest or allow some extra-credit grade for students who draw characters or scenes from *A Wrinkle in Time*. Note, too, that if the students do not want to keep their drawings you may pick up some extra bulletin board materials this way. If you have a contest and you supply the prize (a CD or something like that perhaps), you could, possibly, make the drawing itself a non-returnable entry fee.

The pages which follow contain games, puzzles, and worksheets. The keys, when appropriate, immediately follow the puzzle or worksheet. There are two main groups of activities: one group for the unit; that is, generally relating to *A Wrinkle in Time* text, and another group of activities related strictly to *A Wrinkle in Time* vocabulary.

Directions for these games, puzzles, and worksheets are self-explanatory. The object here is to provide you with extra materials you may use in any way you choose.

MORE ACTIVITIES - *A Wrinkle in Time*

1. Have students design a book cover (front and back and inside flaps) for *A Wrinkle in Time*.

2. Have students design a bulletin board (ready to be put up; not just sketched) for *A Wrinkle in Time*.

3. Have students choose one chapter of the story (with sufficient dialogue) to rewrite as a play. In conjunction with this assignment, have students write a composition explaining the difficulties they encountered in changing from one written form to another.

4. Have students write a sonnet.

5. In conjunction with the writing assignment and reports about the "fighters" have the additional requirement that students must also show some part of the "fighter's" contributions. For example, play a short excerpt from Beethoven's music, listen to or recite a portion of Martin Luther King Jr.'s "I Have a Dream" speech, look at pictures of some of Van Gogh's paintings, etc.

6. Do a group writing assignment to write the plot for a sequel to *A Wrinkle in Time*.

7. Take a trip to a planetarium or have a guest speaker discuss scientific discoveries in space.

8. Do some exercises in communications without words. For example, you could have students take turns doing pantomimes in front of the class.

9. Do exercises in "seeing" without vision. Have students explore all the things that they know and understand but cannot see.

10. Have a day or two devoted to mythology. Have students research some of the most well-known Greek or Roman gods and goddesses and give oral reports about them. Having students dress as their gods adds a fun and interesting element to this activity.

WORD SEARCH - *A Wrinkle in Time*

All words in this list are associated with *A Wrinkle in Time*. The words are placed backwards, forward, diagonally, up and down. The clues below the word search can help you find the words.

```
R R F K B C L O V E N P I N E C G R K F
V G Q V V Z R V H H M X L H J D B G T W
S Y R G T W G S R X J F C R W Y D G B L
Q L Q H L T G L Q P S J C M P K L J L L
D H X C S Q U A R E R O O T N J G Q D Z
N B H Z H F L C F D N B Y T N C D C N K
G J C C N A D E Y Z A Q R J K I M T M V
N E B G Q F R H I V S R X A D R V E D D
T Y N C B B C L W R I N K L E N G L E B
Y E R E Z B P X E X U Q W D Q F I M A Q
A W S L S Y Q W N S Q R R Z V K I T P C
W T D S R I O C V C W U J D E T E Q C K
W H O N E L S P C A M A Z O T Z G V S K
K B I M F R T M K C H Q L P R L W Y I D
G Q S C S K A M N Q Z V B L F L N F B L
Z K G J H L Q C T H T R L L A N R J S K
X X D E C N E I T A P M I P E C O L D J
A U N T B E A S T S Z V Y D B H E Z P Z
```

ATOMS	DARK	LENGLE	URIEL
AUNTBEAST	DENNYS	LIKE	WHICH
CALVIN	EVIL	MEG	WHO
CAMAZOTZ	FEAR	MURDER	WRINKLE
CHARLESWALLACE		FLOWERS	SQUAREROOT
CLOVENPINE	GENESIS	TESSERACT	
COLD	IMPATIENCE	TIME	

CROSSWORD - *A Wrinkle in Time*

CROSSWORD CLUES - *A Wrinkle in Time*

ACROSS
1. Laughing in the _____
2. Short-cut or wrinkle
6. Boy who went with Meg and Charles Wallace
8. Place where IT has won
11. _____ and equal are not the same
13. Ingested food
14. The _____ of 4 is 2
16. The line of intersection of two surfaces; rim
17. Recurring, often unconsciously, pattern of behavior
18. Small particles
21. Present singular of 'to be'
22. Gives Meg her love
24. She saves Charles Wallace
25. Planet where they rested
27. Author
31. Opportunity
32. Tesseract
33. Acquires

DOWN
1. A twin
2. A Wrinkle in ____
3. Halt
4. She did confine thee into a ____
5. It
7. Meg's Ixchel friend
8. Meg's brother
9. A most primitive word; kill
10. Meg's after tessering temperature
12. One of Meg's faults
15. They made breathing possible
19. Make wider
20. She talks in quotations
23. Feeling towards the Dark Thing
26. First book of the Bible
28. Mild mannered; kind
29. Present plural of 'to be'
30. Coordinating conjunction

CROSSWORD ANSWER KEY - *A Wrinkle in Time*

					D	A	R	K			T	E	S	S	E	R	A	C	T
			E		E						I		T				L		
C	A	L	V	I	N			C	A	M	A	Z	O	T	Z		O		
	U		I		N			H		E			P				V		
	N		L		Y	M	A			C				L	I	K	E		
A	T	E			S	Q	U	A	R	E	R	O	O	T		M		N	
	B		F			R		L			L				P		P		
	E		L		E	D	G	E			D		H	A	B	I	T		
	A	T	O	M	S		E	S		W		W			T		N		
I	S		W		R		W	H	I	C	H				I		E		
	T		E		F		A		D		O		M	E	G				
		U	R	I	E	L		L		E		G		N					
			S		A			L	E	N	G	L	E		C				
					R			A			E		N		E				
			A		A		C	H	A	N	C	E							
			W	R	I	N	K	L	E		T		S						
			E		D				T		L		I						
								G	E	T	S								

MATCHING QUIZ/WORKSHEET 1 - *A Wrinkle in Time*

____ 1. SQUAREROOT   A. Meg's after tessering temperature

____ 2. WRINKLE   B. Tesseract

____ 3. COLD   C. Planet where they rested

____ 4. CHARLESWALLACE   D. She saves Charles Wallace

____ 5. GENESIS   E. Meg's brother

____ 6. IMPATIENCE   F. Meg's Ixchel friend

____ 7. CAMAZOTZ   G. Place where IT has won

____ 8. CLOVENPINE   H. Short-cut or wrinkle

____ 9. TESSERACT   I. The _____ of 4 is 2

____ 10. MURDER   J. Author

____ 11. ATOMS   K. She did confine thee into a _____

____ 12. DARK   L. First book of the Bible

____ 13. LIKE   M. She talks in quotations

____ 14. FEAR   N. A most primitive word; kill

____ 15. CALVIN   O. Feeling towards the Dark Thing

____ 16. AUNTBEAST   P. Laughing in the _____

____ 17. LENGLE   Q. Small particles

____ 18. WHO   R. Boy who went with Meg and Charles Wallace

____ 19. URIEL   S. _____ and equal are not the same

____ 20. MEG   T. One of Meg's faults

MATCHING QUIZ/WORKSHEET 2 - *A Wrinkle in Time*

____ 1. ATOMS   A. Meg's Ixchel friend

____ 2. DENNYS   B. They made breathing possible

____ 3. AUNTBEAST   C. A Wrinkle in ____

____ 4. FEAR   D. She did confine thee into a _____

____ 5. IMPATIENCE   E. Gives Meg her love

____ 6. WHO   F. A twin

____ 7. GENESIS   G. Meg's after tessering temperature

____ 8. LENGLE   H. Place where IT has won

____ 9. CLOVENPINE   I. First book of the Bible

____ 10. TESSERACT   J. A most primitive word; kill

____ 11. WRINKLE   K. One of Meg's faults

____ 12. MURDER   L. Tesseract

____ 13. TIME   M. Feeling towards the Dark Thing

____ 14. COLD   N. Author

____ 15. CHARLESWALLACE   O. She talks in quotations

____ 16. DARK   P. Small particles

____ 17. FLOWERS   Q. It

____ 18. CAMAZOTZ   R. Laughing in the _____

____ 19. EVIL   S. Short-cut or wrinkle

____ 20. WHICH   T. Meg's brother

KEY: MATCHING QUIZ/WORKSHEETS - *A Wrinkle in Time*

Worksheet 1
1. I
2. B
3. A
4. E
5. L
6. T
7. G
8. K
9. H
10. N
11. Q
12. P
13. S
14. O
15. R
16. F
17. J
18. M
19. C
20. D

Worksheet 2
1. P
2. F
3. A
4. M
5. K
6. O
7. I
8. N
9. D
10. S
11. L
12. J
13. C
14. G
15. T
16. R
17. B
18. H
19. Q
20. E

JUGGLE LETTER REVIEW GAME CLUE SHEET - *A Wrinkle in Time*

SCRAMBLED	WORD	CLUE
STAMO	ATOMS	Small particles
BUNTSEATA	AUNTBEAST	Meg's Ixchel friend
VALINC	CALVIN	Boy who went with Meg and Charles Wallace
ZATAMOCZ	CAMAZOTZ	Place where IT has won
RLAEHCS	CHARLES	____ Wallace
NINLOVPECE	CLOVENPINE	She did confine thee into a _____
CLOD	COLD	Meg's after tessering temperature
KARD	DARK	Laughing in the _____
NYSEND	DENNYS	A twin
LIVE	EVIL	It
REAF	FEAR	Feeling towards the Dark Thing
WOLFERS	FLOWERS	They made breathing possible
SEGSNSI	GENESIS	First book of the Bible
PENTACIMIE	IMPATIENCE	One of Meg's faults
GELNEL	LENGLE	Author
KILE	LIKE	_____ and equal are not the same
GME	MEG	She saves Charles Wallace
REDRUM	MURDER	A most primitive word; kill
QUOTARSOER	SQUAREROOT	The _____ of 4 is 2
STARSETEC	TESSERACT	Short-cut or wrinkle
LURIE	URIEL	Planet where they rested
CHIHW	WHICH	Gives Meg her love
HOW	WHO	She talks in quotations
KLIRENW	WRINKLE	Tesseract
MITE	TIME	A Wrinkle in ____

VOCABULARY RESOURCE MATERIALS

VOCABULARY WORD SEARCH - *A Wrinkle in Time*

All words in this list are associated with the vocabulary from *A Wrinkle in Time*. The words are placed backwards, forward, diagonally, up and down. The clues below the word searches can help you find the words.

```
A S S I M I L A T E Z N N Q Z T V A A C U T E A
D X R T X A S Q N Q G K T S G D Y R N O C R S N
R X F M Z R L C D N R D Q N E S S B M G U S V P
P E R M E A T I N G I F I T N E V I R T U E S M
D R I F Y T S Q G V N H A B I G N T S A P I I S
B K E T C P A T A N T N I R L O Z E G H Y S S E
B D R S E R M M H A A S A L U R G E E N C O G H
D S R R E R E F O M B N F S A D D M U O M R H T
S U S E Z N A L E R I S T J E T E P N N O S P B
N E B I A L T T B M P Q U C Y R E C I G A R S T
D O H I L S H M I A U H Y R A T E P I W O U X Z
O P N I O B S L E N R G O L D P O N K P O P Y N
T B B D V U E U O N G T A S T T E C I I H R T W
F L L Y E R S B R T T I E I E X A T C T U E C B
E U S I P S S L D A R D O N O B I I Q F Y Y R X
N Q R H Q C C Y Y E N N T R E O V H K M K L G N
D G C T U U C R T T N C A N U P I N V E R T E D
H F S R I H E S I H F B E S S R M B R W Y Q J X
Q W E V L V Y L X P L A P P A L L I N G L Y M C
H D K R N H E F Y E T I N D I G N A T I O N Z T
```

ABSURD	DEFT	INDIGNATION	PRELIMINARIES
ACUTE	DISPERSED	INEXORABLE	PROPITIOUS
ANGUISH	DUBIOUSLY	INVERTED	PUNY
ANNIHILATE	EMANATED	LOATHING	REASSURANCE
APPALLINGLY	EPHEMERAL	MALIGNANT	REITERATING
ASSIMILATE	FALLIBLE	METAMORPHOSE	RESENTMENT
ASSUAGED	FURTIVE	MISCONCEPTION	SERENITY
AVID	FURY	NONDESCRIPT	UNOBSCURED
BACKWASH	GESTURE	OBLIQUELY	VICIOUS
BLISS	GORGE	OMINOUS	VIRTUES
DECIPHER	HYSTERIA	OMNIPOTENT	
DEFER	IMPENETRABLE	PERMEATING	

VOCABULARY CROSSWORD - *A Wrinkle in Time*

VOCABULARY CROSSWORD CLUES - *A Wrinkle in Time*

ACROSS
1. Gives Meg her love
5. To absorb or incorporate
9. Not obstructed; in full view
11. Those who secretly keep watch on others
12. Unintentionally; by accident
16. A motion of the limbs or body
17. Take action
20. Sharp; severe
21. A Wrinkle in ____
22. Spiteful; malicious
25. She saves Charles Wallace
26. Makes a dent in; also, they mark paragraphs
28. Small
29. Meg's after tessering temperature
31. Loud
32. A mass obstructing a narrow passage
34. Nasty; cruel
35. Rage; violent anger
36. Agonizing physical or mental pain
38. Good qualities
39. Feeling towards the Dark Thing
43. Can make mistakes
45. Decode; to read or interpret
46. Laughing in the _____
47. A twin

DOWN
1. She talks in quotations
2. Indignation or ill-will felt as a result of some offense
3. Abated; settled down; lessened
4. Put off to a later time
6. Tranquility
7. Belonging to me
8. Dread; uneasy anticipation
10. Serene happiness
13. Doubtfully
14. An extreme dislike
15. Preparations
18. Author
19. Enthusiastic; ardent
20. Made less severe
23. Comfortingly; seeking or giving in confidence
24. Short-lived; lasting only a short time
27. Stealthy
30. Skillful
33. Turned upside down or wrong side out
36. Ridiculous
37. Planet where they rested
40. _____ and equal are not the same
41. Plot; scheme
42. It
43. Opposite of near
44. Definite article

VOCABULARY CROSSWORD ANSWER KEY - *A Wrinkle in Time*

VOCABULARY WORKSHEET 1 *A Wrinkle in Time*

____ 1. Tranquility
    A. Reiterating   B. Serenity   C. Inverted   D. Absurd

____ 2. Abated; settled down; lessened
    A. Simultaneously   B. Malignant   C. Subsided   D. Absurd

____ 3. Excessive or uncontrollable fear or other emotions
    A. Assuaged   B. Annihilate   C. Hysteria   D. Vicious

____ 4. Good qualities
    A. Annihilate   B. Appallingly   C. Virtues   D. Inverted

____ 5. At the same time
    A. Serenity   B. Simultaneously   C. Impenetrable   D. Deft

____ 6. Incorrect understanding
    A. Dubiously   B. Misconception   C. Unadulterated   D. Dispersed

____ 7. Made less severe
    A. Assuaged   B. Assimilate   C. Inexorable   D. Puny

____ 8. Doubtfully
    A. Vicious   B. Indignation   C. Unadulterated   D. Dubiously

____ 9. Unyielding
    A. Hysteria   B. Virtues   C. Backwash   D. Inexorable

____ 10. Preparations
    A. Vicious   B. Malignant   C. Preliminaries   D. Permeating

____ 11. Can't be gone through
    A. Puny   B. Impenetrable   C. Unadulterated   D. Inverted

____ 12. A mass obstructing a narrow passage
    A. Emanated   B. Annihilate   C. Gorge   D. Vicious

____ 13. Put off to a later time
    A. Furtive   B. Absurd   C. Defer   D. Gorge

____ 14. Not obstructed; in full view
    A. Resentment   B. Unobscured   C. Indignation   D. Hysteria

____ 15. To absorb or incorporate
    A. Fallible   B. Unobscured   C. Assimilate   D. Obliquely

____ 16. Decode; to read or interpret
    A. Malignant   B. Dubiously   C. Decipher   D. Anguish

____ 17. Comfortingly; seeking or giving in confidence
    A. Confidingly   B. Simultaneously   C. Backwash   D. Puny

____ 18. Unbearable
    A. Intolerable   B. Serenity   C. Reiterating   D. Practicable

____ 19. Evil in nature
    A. Malignant   B. Belligerent   C. Absurd   D. Acute

____ 20. Sharp; severe
    A. Acute   B. Nondescript   C. Inadvertently   D. Assuaged

VOCABULARY WORKSHEET 2 - *A Wrinkle in Time*

____ 1. BLISS   A. Can't be gone through

____ 2. AVID   B. Stealthy

____ 3. PRACTICABLE   C. Unintentionally; by accident

____ 4. UNADULTERATED D. Not diluted; pure

____ 5. ASSIMILATE   E. Can be done; feasible

____ 6. ANNIHILATE   F. Indignation or ill-will felt as a result of some offense

____ 7. INADVERTENTLY G. Presenting favorable circumstances

____ 8. RESENTMENT   H. Decode; to read or interpret

____ 9. PROPITIOUS   I. Saying or doing the same thing again

____ 10. REITERATING J. To absorb or incorporate

____ 11. GESTURE   K. Wipe out; totally destroy

____ 12. INEXORABLE   L. Not obstructed; in full view

____ 13. APPALLINGLY M. A motion of the limbs or body

____ 14. SUBSIDED   N. Abated; settled down; lessened

____ 15. FURTIVE   O. Short-lived; lasting only a short time

____ 16. EPHEMERAL   P. Unyielding

____ 17. IMPENETRABLE Q. Causing dismay

____ 18. DECIPHER   R. Put off to a later time

____ 19. UNOBSCURED   S. Serene happiness

____ 20. DEFER   T. Enthusiastic; ardent

KEY: VOCABULARY WORKSHEETS - *A Wrinkle in Time*

Worksheet 1	Worksheet 2
1. B	1. S
2. C	2. T
3. C	3. E
4. C	4. D
5. B	5. J
6. B	6. K
7. A	7. C
8. D	8. F
9. D	9. G
10. C	10. I
11. B	11. M
12. C	12. P
13. C	13. Q
14. B	14. N
15. C	15. B
16. C	16. O
17. A	17. A
18. A	18. H
19. A	19. L
20. A	20. R

VOCABULARY JUGGLE LETTER REVIEW GAME - *A Wrinkle in Time*

Scrambled	Word	Definition
CIOIVSU	VICIOUS	Spiteful; malicious
TYRESINE	SERENITY	Tranquility
MLINERASIREPI	PRELIMINARIES	Preparations
NESTMEENTR	RESENTMENT	Indignation or ill-will felt as a result of some offense
TEGRESU	GESTURE	A motion of the limbs or body
DAVI	AVID	Enthusiastic; ardent
FDGONYLINIC	CONFIDINGLY	Comfortingly; seeking or giving in confidence
VEETDINYNRTAL	INADVERTENTLY	Unintentionally; by accident
AGINTINNODI	INDIGNATION	Anger aroused by something mean or unjust
ASMALETISI	ASSIMILATE	To absorb or incorporate
CHEPIRED	DECIPHER	Decode; to read or interpret
SBULYODUI	DUBIOUSLY	Doubtfully
FEDT	DEFT	Skillful
OXENBRALIE	INEXORABLE	Unyielding
MEPRHELAE	EPHEMERAL	Short-lived; lasting only a short time PE-
SHONPANERI	APPREHENSION	Dread; uneasy anticipation
MOOSEATHPEMR	METAMORPHOSE	Change in form; transform
SLIBS	BLISS	Serene happiness
PEDISDERS	DISPERSED	Became less dense by scattering; dispelled
DUBSNURECO	UNOBSCURED	Not obstructed; in full view
KCHABWAS	BACKWASH	Backward flow of air, as from a propeller
LISTONOSDUI	DISSOLUTION	Decomposition into fragments or parts
BORTELEANIL	INTOLERABLE	Unbearable
SEDBDISU	SUBSIDED	Abated; settled down; lessened
LANMGINAT	MALIGNANT	Evil in nature
ORPISOUPIT	PROPITIOUS	Presenting favorable circumstances
UTEVIRF	FURTIVE	Stealthy
NSACRUEEARS	REASSURANCE	Something that restores confidence
CNNDIPTREOS	NONDESCRIPT	Ordinary; has no outstanding features
QUYLBILEO	OBLIQUELY	At a slant
TRESUIV	VIRTUES	Good qualities
RFYU	FURY	Rage; violent anger
LENGEBLIERT	BELLIGERENT	Marked by hostile behavior
RYTEASHI	HYSTERIA	Excessive or uncontrollable fear or other emotions
POCCNONISEITM	MISCONCEPTION	Incorrect understanding
NITHINALAE	ANNIHILATE	Wipe out; totally destroy
MOONIUS	OMINOUS	Foreboding; Signaling something bad
PERNBLETEMIA	IMPENETRABLE	Can't be gone through

Wrinkle Review Game Continued

FEDER	DEFER	Put off to a later time
GHINUAS	ANGUISH	Agonizing physical or mental pain
RINEDTEV	INVERTED	Turned upside down or wrong side out
CRATELBAPIC	PRACTICABLE	Can be done; feasible
YUNP	PUNY	Small
PONITOMNET	OMNIPOTENT	All powerful
LILEBALF	FALLIBLE	Can make mistakes
SAEGDUAS	ASSUAGED	Made less severe
TUECA	ACUTE	Sharp; severe
EGGOR	GORGE	A mass obstructing a narrow passage
RUSDBA	ABSURD	Ridiculous
METADEAN	EMANATED	Originated; came from
GLAYLIPLANP	APPALLINGLY	Causing dismay
TLUSLNEYMAOSIU	SIMULTANEOUSLY	At the same time
PINTAMEREG	PERMEATING	Spreading or flowing throughout
TAREREINGIT	REITERATING	Saying or doing the same thing again
TOALGHIN	LOATHING	An extreme dislike
RETDULTEDNAUA	UNADULTERATED	Not diluted; pure

www.ingramcontent.com/pod-product-compliance
Lightning Source LLC
Chambersburg PA
CBHW051418070526
44584CB00023B/3478